The 90 Day Yacht Club
Guide to Ensenada

Captain Lonnie Ryan

A True Traveler Publication

The 90 Day Yacht Club Guide to Ensenada
By Lonnie Ryan

Published by:

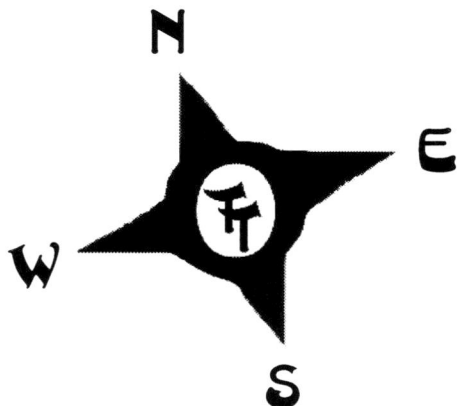

TRUE TRAVELER PUBLISHING

Post Office Box 60023
San Diego, CA 92166 U.S.A.
www.truetraveler.com

Publishers Cataloging In Publication
by Lonnie Ryan-1st edition
          p.   cm.
Includes index.
ISBN 0-9726690-1-9
The 90 day yacht club guide to Ensenada
1. Ensenada (Baja California, Mexico)--Guidebooks I. Title
2. Yachts and yachting
3. Tax havens
F1246.R95
917.223-dc20   2002096092 CIP

Disclaimer

WARNING: The descriptions, waypoints and navigation data included in this text are intended as only an aid to navigation. Final decisions and trip planning as to the navigation of the vessel are the responsibility of the owner, captain and/or crew. The maps and drawings in this text are not replacements for the use of authorized government charts. Only official government charts and notices to mariners contain all the information needed for the safety of navigation, and as always, the user is responsible for their prudent use. The author and publisher of this book in no way, stated or implied, warrant the contents of the book to be error free.

DO NOT USE THE DRAWINGS IN THIS BOOK FOR NAVIGATION. TRUE TRAVELER PUBLISHING, THE AUTHOR, AND THE VENDOR THAT SUPPLIES THIS PUBLICATION ARE IN NO WAY RESPONSIBLE FOR LOSS OR DAMAGE DUE TO THE USE OF THIS BOOK.

An Important Message to Our Readers

This product provides information and general advice about the law. But laws and procedures change frequently, and they can be interpreted differently by different people. For specific advice geared to your specific situation, consult an expert. No book, software or other published material is a substitute for personalized advice from a knowledgeable lawyer licensed to practice in your state.

If you do not wish to be bound by the above, you may return this book to the publisher for a full refund.

Please Contact Us

We would appreciate your response and continued feedback about your experiences while traveling in Mexico using our book. Legal issues and the method of offshore delivery are true to the best of our knowledge through direct experience, but policies by our government agencies change daily and may affect the future of your eligibility for successful 90 Day Yacht Club results. We wrote this book with this maxim in mind, "give the people the most amount of information in the least amount of time." You can contact us at truetraveler.com. Thank you for your patronage of this book. Above all, we hope you will enjoy traveling through the areas of Mexico described in this book before they too are spoiled by overpopulation.

Buena Suerte!

Table of Contents

A true traveler has no fixed plans and is not intent upon arrival...

Author's Note

W e hope you enjoy reading about, and profit from, our experience. Like most authors, our writing days either came naturally or were a product of intense self-prodding. Overriding the call to create chapters was the endearment we feel and hope to convey for the cultural beauty of the Mexican lifestyle.

There exists an innocent attitude toward new technology, a technology as yet unrealized by the majority of the people inhabiting this evolving Latino State. Many families live without items we take for granted as common place in our homes; electricity, running water, televisions, video players, computers and video games. Rather than take advantage of this innocence by only exploiting cheap labor and using the Baja as a weekend vacation, the United States would be well served by developing brotherhood between two neighboring States, which still to this day share the title of California, by investing in the education and enrichment of future Baja generations.

We take every opportunity to bring with us household appliances, bicycles, children's toys, scooters, used computers, clothing, etc., to give to those we know who have little to show for the many years dedicated to raising a family in somewhat primitive and simple circumstances. The time spent collecting the unused and discarded items of worth in your neighborhood will be returned to you within the smiles of those less fortunate as these gifts are given. The marina dock security personnel that help you tie up your new x-number of dollars mega-yacht earn around US 60$ a week while raising a family. We make sure a few dollars go their way when their willing help is given. Whether presented as a tip or a gift, it may make an unexpected surprise within the family possible that may otherwise not be shared.

As an emerging country, the pride shared in a history replete with revolution and a class struggle to survive will bring this group of hard workers a greater prosperity and a higher education for future generations. Your help to make this evolution a reality will enrich your time spent in Mexico while at the 90 Day Yacht Club.

Introduction

This book is the result of the author's membership at the 90 Day Yacht Club. Captain Lonnie Ryan has been in Mexico for 4 years, commuting to and from his sailboat at Marina Coral near Ensenada. Captain Ryan was instrumental in facilitating the delivery of boats, commissioning and equipping a number of boats for offshore delivery, having made the trip between Ensenada and San Diego over 150 times. During his life he has been traveling to, and exploring Mexico for over 35 years. Captain Ryan is an accomplished seaman, having spent 2 years on a National Oceanographic and Atmospheric Administration (NOAA) ship as an Electronic Technician. He was in charge of shipboard operations and small boat exploration away from the ship performing tide survey data collection in the Columbia River and the San Francisco Bay. He has delivered yachts throughout Mexico and navigated his own boat in California and Mexican waters. He is a holder of a First Class Federal Communications license and a 100 ton Coast Guard issued Captain's license. This book was written in the Captain's mind long before it came to print and is a result of meetings with visiting boaters, whose many questions about their offshore delivery experience propelled this book to the reality of the written word. As new members of the 90 Day Yacht Club, the boaters relied on Lonnie to answer their questions and concerns about successful implementation of the offshore delivery process. The results are these chapters of hopefully helpful information to make realization of your tax exemption an easy and enjoyable task. A book on this subject has long been needed and we now present it to you with answers to those questions you may have about your offshore experience.

This book will help you enjoy a cost savings of the 7%+ California State Tax on the purchase price of your boat. This savings on a yacht sale may help buy a larger boat, make the buyer's offer more flexible, or make the down payment funds available for approval of financing. You may want to use the savings to update the electronics, mechanics, or cosmetics on your new boat. While in Ensenada you may be able to do some needed work in one of the boat yards implementing improvements on your new yacht that are overdue.

We know your investment in this book will return rewards far beyond your tax savings. It is our aspiration that the suggestions of how to spend time while at the 90 Day Yacht Club will also make the purchase of your new boat and time spent offshore more enjoyable.

A Letter of Welcome

To Lonnie Ryan
Author of The 90 Day Yacht Club Guide to Ensenada

Dear Mr. Ryan,

On behalf of the Ensenada Convention and Tourism Bureau, we wish to extend a most cordial welcome and "Bienvenidos" to all your friends coming our way. Our offices are located just to the right of the first stop light entering Ensenada. Our staff will be glad to provide any information needed to make their visit a most happy one. We wish to congratulate you for providing accurate information to our friends visiting Baja California and especially Ensenada.

Saludos y Hasta Pronto,

Nico Saad
Vice President of Special Events

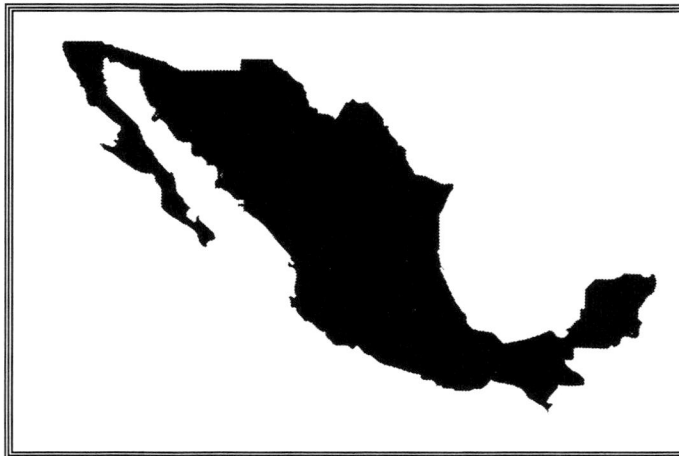

Notes and Remembrances

Why Ensenada?

This question reminds us of the old adage; location, location, location. The proximity of Ensenada is most convenient for those living in the Western United States. We have met many boaters from as far north as San Francisco who have realized that a 7%+ savings on their boat is a big savings and that the cost of transporting their new boat between their location and the 90 Day Yacht Club is negligible when compared to the benefits received, which include quality family time spent celebrating the new floating addition to the family. A mere 1 hour and 30 minute drive and 90 miles from San Diego will enable you to escape the smog, overcrowded confusion and hoards of cell phone grafted to the ear trend followers. You, my friend, are about to become a trend setter. The fishing stories told around Mexican campfires and in offshore delivery boat galleys are real and not imagined. Last week a neighbor across the docks from us brought in a big eye tuna that weighed 200 lbs. plus and was the size of a VW bug door, landed during a 60 mile round trip. That was only one of the 40 or so fish including albacore, dorado, and yellowtail landed that day. This is one of the two boats on the docks owned by an American friend, legally available for charter. Although this book is intended to educate those planning to take advantage of the 90 day offshore delivered tax-exempt yacht sale, we hope it will also be of help to those simply wishing to enjoy the attractions of Ensenada, by boat or by car.

Right now a live band is serenading us up at the Marina Coral pool, projecting throughout the Marina as we sit in the cockpit of our sailboat writing this text. Waves can be heard breaking on the jetty that surrounds our snug Pacific enclave. It is an August day and while the rest of the Northern Hemisphere swelters in humid heat, it is a perfect breeze cooled 73 degrees here on the docks. I am reminded of the huge mid-winter waves crashing with deep percussion on the jetty, creating sparkling waterfalls on the rocks as the foam is thrown over the rock partition between the often-violent Pacific Ocean and our sheltered man made cove. The night skies are free of smog, laden with stars and perfectly quiet. Only the sound of the tiny denizens that move about our hull in the murky silence of our little marina sea is heard, occasionally punctuated by the squawk of a long legged crane taking flight.

After a bit more of today's exercise in avoiding writer's cramp, a veranda at the hotel overlooking the pool offers a cool refreshment and a view with a sweeping vista of the Bahia Todos Santos. These are some of the most immediate answers we have discovered as to "Why Ensenada?". We hope you will benefit further as we present more answers to your questions in the chapters to come.

The Fear Factor

As humans, we possess a natural fear of that which we do not understand. Also, as humans we often do things we would prefer not to do if the money is good enough. The ideal situation before embarking to the 90 Day Yacht Club is that your fears are reduced and the choices are made through a previous local knowledge of the area, enabling the benefit in savings to be the determining factor in your decision. This is one of the reasons we are writing this book for you. We hope the overall cause and effect of this text is to reassure your decision to make the offshore delivery a well made decision, and for you to enjoy the days spent in manana-land, and your resultant tax savings.

The isolated stories you have heard or read of misfortune experienced by others have been the result of bad judgment, poor preparation, and/or a bit of bad luck. Driving in Mexico after consuming alcohol or drugs is not advised. In addition, any possession of firearms in Mexico is strictly prohibited. Your drive to and from Ensenada may include a checkpoint for firearms and drugs search and seizure. The majority of times through these checkpoints you will be waved on through, however, at times a search may be performed. Your attitude is very important when dealing with any form of authority in Mexico. A smile and an attempt at what little Spanish you may speak will go a long way toward determining the treatment you receive from the Mexican authorities. This may determine if you are lightly searched or all your belongings searched in earnest.

When crossing the border there is the famous red light/green light system determining whether you are subject to search for imported goods or allowed to cruise through. A red light and loud bell will be your cue to pull to the right and into the inspection lanes. Again, attitude is important if inspected. Have the original copy of your importation document issued when checked into the port of Ensenada with you. If you are importing a lot of boat gear, this may allow you through without paying importation duties. But that document is not a guarantee of you not paying importation duties; this is subject to the mood of, and interpretation of the law, subject to the discretion of the inspecting official. Our best advise is a friendly greeting by you and a willingness to open every door when asked. Don't willfully offer information about what you have, your destination, or your possession of the importation documentation, except when asked. Also, try to keep importation of new gear to a minimum. The Mexican border officials would have you pull into the "Declare" lanes automatically, but this could be costly in time and funds. A part of your pre-trip planning would have all that great new stuff from your local marine store already on the boat when disembarking from the U.S.. But forgotten or upgrade items may have to be transported during your 90 day stay. Remember to smile and learn to say "Holla, como esta usted?" ("hello, how are you"), etc... in Spanish to lessen the tension and put you back on the road to the 90 Day Yacht Club (see our Spanish glossary for more useful phrases).

Once more, do not drink and drive, possess firearms or drugs, and most importantly cop an attitude if stopped or searched. The ugly American image is not wanted south of the border and Mexican citizens can sense that attitude immediately. A measure of mutual respect and common sense, along with local knowledge of the area will go a long way to help lessen the Fear Factor.

Ensenada History

In 1542 Juan Rodriguez Cabrillo first sailed into this bay, that in 1602 Sebastian Vizcaino named Ensenada-Bahia de Todos Santos (All Saints' Bay). Since then, the town has seen a succession of "discoverers" and developers. In the 17th century, the bay was used for shelter both by the Manila galleons and the pirates lying in wait for them. The ensuing years saw little local activity aside from the cattle ranchers who made their homes on expansive rancheros on the coast and into the surrounding mountains.

It's interesting to note that there is no missionary-built church in this area. Gold, not God, developed the area into what is now known as a town. Ambrosio Castillo discovered the first nuggets in 1872, which signaled the beginning of the boomtown era as gold rush fever brought new settlers from other areas. Now becoming a center of trade and support for the miners, with all the graft and greed that are usually a result, Ensenada endured the effects of this sudden prosperity. In 1882, Ensenada was appointed capital of the territory. By the late 1880's the mines were depleted and the area returned to its previous pastoral existence. The town's population of 1400 consisted of primarily out-of-luck miners.

The next decade saw the development of huge tracts of land charter in the south near San Quintin by British and American holding companies headquartered in Ensenada. At the turn of the century, the capital appointment was lost to Mexicali and the Mexican Revolution of 1915 annulled these land charters.

Gradually the harbor grew into a major seaport and became an export center for the agricultural goods of Valle de Mexicali. Being the closest foreign port to California, the town and surrounding ranches and farms enjoyed a renewed period of growth and wealth.

When the 1930's emerged as the era of bootleg liquor, smuggling activities and gambling establishments became a staple of the economy. At the corner of Blvd. Lazaro Cardenas and Ave. Riviera is the former Casino Riviera del Pacifico, built in the late 1920's. In it's heyday it was a famous gambling house, once managed by the boxer Jack Dempsey. The opening act in 1929 featured Bing Crosby backed by the Xavier Cugat Orchestra. The orchestra included a singer named Margarita Carmen Cansino, a Baja native later to be known as Rita Hayworth. It now can be visited in its current incarnation as a cultural center.

For a period of time Ensenada became a little Havana, but the legalization of liquor in the U.S. in 1933 and the outlawing of gambling in Mexico in 1938 meant the end of these sordid times.

Throughout the 1940s and '50s the port gained a reputation as one of the finest sport and commercial fishing areas on the west coast, having at one time been known as the "Yellowtail Capital of the World". In an effort to attract more tourism dollars, the downtown waterfront has been redeveloped and a new cruise ship terminal constructed. Three yacht marinas, with all the conveniences expected in California marinas have been built. As the third largest city in Baja and unofficial capital of Mexico's finest wine-producing area, this bustling city continues to attract those wishing to experience a taste of traditional old Mexico. Hussong's Cantina, serving as a reminder of the area's frontier days has changed little over the years.

A part of the Ensenada allure is its tendency to be event driven, rather than relying on specific sites of tourism. We enjoy annual celebrations; which include Carnival, Cinco de Mayo, wine festivals, surfing contests, sailboat races, fishing tournaments, off-road car races, and the migration of the gray whale. If your schedule permits we suggest a more sedate mid-week visit as this area is either a busy tourist center or a small quiet town, dependant on whether you visit on a Saturday or a Wednesday.

Our ecological advice while visiting Mexico is:

"Take only photos and leave only footprints."

And remember, the beautiful sea that surrounds us and nurtures our very existence is neither an ashtray or a trashcan.

The Drive To and From Ensenada

One of the best features of your Mexico experience is the wonderful modern 4-lane toll road from Tijuana to Ensenada. This road is designated Highway 1D, the D indicating directo in Spanish. There are three toll plazas between these points and you can choose to take the entire route which will cost you between $2 and $2.50 per toll plaza, depending on the exchange rate. Service vehicles patrol the road and there are free road assistance phones along the way for you to use if you need help. Each toll area has clean bathrooms at the exit of the tollbooths in both directions. If time permits, stop and enjoy the hill, which is home to a large number of very active squirrels at the exit of the Rosarito northbound tollbooths, next to the little convenience store.

If you are not in a hurry and possess an adventurous spirit, the entire toll road can be averted, as there is a two lane free road which can be slower, but far more interesting. This route is designated Highway 1. You will be traveling through a collection of roadside businesses that include pottery, iron sculpture, furniture, tile, and art shops. A wealth of hotels, restaurants, and liquor stores will be found along this route. A tour of the studios where the movie Titanic was filmed is along this free road to Ensenada. Many exits are provided on the toll road to the parallel free road and you can access these locations by observing the well-marked signs at these exits. Calafia, the Halfway house, and La Mision are suggested stops en route to Ensenada. Puerto Nuevo, where rows of lobster-serving restaurants can be found, has been a favorite stop for many years. One price per person will bring you a platter of tasty lobster and all the rice, beans, and tortillas you can eat. Night or day these roads are safe and well patrolled by safety vehicles and police units. A distance of approximately 70 miles is covered from the USA/Mexican border enroute to the 90 Day Yacht Club, and can be traveled in roughly one hour and 30 minutes from San Diego, if you drive carefully and obey the speed limits.

If you prefer to travel the road that has served for decades as the free road to Ensenada and pay no tolls, here are your directions. See our maps included later in this text, which illustrate your road passage to and from Ensenada. Immediately after crossing the border heading south and as you subsequently cross the long bridge over the dry riverbed, get in the extreme right hand lane, which will feed you down to an off ramp and onto the street Paseo De Los Heroes. You are now on a street with 6 lanes divided by a wide, fenced, center tree lined island. At the second light, you will pass a McDonald's restaurant on the right and you will navigate through a European style round intersection. Go straight thru this intersection, bearing to the right around the circle, paying attention to those who may want to continue to the left, sometimes crossing in front of you. Negotiating these round intersections can be challenging so just take it slow and keep a 360 degree watch on those vehicles around you. You are now approaching your right hand turn onto the free road to Ensenada. On your left is a large shopping center marked by a large vertical theater marquee listing more than a dozen movies, and on your right will be a very tall mirrored building. Next you will pass a large orange restaurant on your right and you will be approaching a shorter Bancomer bank mirrored building. You will see a large green sign (somewhat shrouded by trees at a distance) suspended in front of this mirrored building on the corner reading "Ensenada" with an arrow pointing right. This is your right hand turn. As you turn right you will see a small white sign on the opposite corner of your new street to the right marked "Ensenada Libre". One block after turning, you will approach a light, which will feed you onto a slight left dogleg and to another light. Passing through this light, you will now find yourself on a one-way three-lane road, which soon becomes a two-way four-lane road. You will now continue on this same road up a hill past a military camp, the La Gloria exit and over the top of the hill. You will now see the sea as you drop down the hill into Rosarito, and if it is a clear day, you will be afforded a buena vista of the Coronado Islands. You will now have to decide if you want to continue on the free road or transfer to the toll road at the interchange where the toll road passes underneath the free road. We usually choose to do a half-and-half route by taking the short cut over the hills of Tijuana and onto the toll road at Rosarito, and just before the Rosarito toll plaza, we exit at the Las Rocas exit, travel the free road to the onramp at Raul's sports bar, just before Puerto Nuevo. This method passes two toll plazas and you only pay at the San Miguel plaza at the termination of the toll road. If you choose to bypass this last toll plaza and pay no tolls for the entire trip, you can exit at La Mision, and you will be taken through the mountains on the old two lane free road and be deposited back on the main road to Ensenada just after the San Miguel toll plaza.

Back to the border again traveling south: If you choose to travel the toll road and breeze the whole way without traffic stops other than the tollbooths, here is your route. After crossing the border and the bridge over the dry riverbed, stay to the left and take the circle exit (the second circle exit) marked "Ensenada Scenic Road" that circles around to the left and onto a road that travels along the border fence and feeds you onto the toll road as you leave the downtown Tijuana area. Simply staying on the toll road will find you an hour and 10 minutes later, and a few dollars lighter, in Ensenada.

The northern route is the reverse of the southerly set of directions. We choose to pay the first toll at San Miguel and travel to the off ramp just after Puerto Nuevo at Raul's sports bar and join the free road there. Then we travel the free road past the Fox Studios, and just after the roadside businesses entering Rosarito, and beyond the Rosarito toll plaza on your right, get back on the toll road. The exit after you pass the exit marked Col Constitucion is an off ramp marked "La Gloria/Tijuana Libre" which is the free road back over the hill to Tijuana and the border. As you drop down the hill into Tijuana, you will find yourself on a three lane one-way street which travels one block parallel to the road you took going south. At the base of the hill you will bear to the right through an intersection and two blocks later will find you at a circle intersection marked by a large statue of a warrior with a feather headdress. Continuing around this circle to the left will cause you to left hand turn onto the same street you were on coming south, Paseo De Los Heroes. The large shopping center will now be on your right and passing straight through the circle intersection with the McDonalds now on your left will feed you onto the bridge over the dry riverbed and to the lanes entering the border crossing booths.

*A border crossing tip: Get into the most extreme right hand lanes as these lanes divide into other lanes as you approach the border and the crossing booths and therefore move much faster.

We have a second route north we use if advisories heard on the morning radio reports on radio AM 600 indicate a lengthy border wait at Tijuana. Just after passing thru the little town of El Sauzal, just west of Ensenada, there is an exit at an overpass marked Tecate. This is right after passing under a pedestrian only bridge and while passing the fish processing plant to your left. The road to Tecate takes you inland through wineries, mountains, and rural Mexican villages. It's a free two-lane road, designated Highway 3, which offers scenery completely different from that of the coast route. This route is almost exactly the same distance and time to the border and usually you will find no more than a 5 to 10 car wait through one lane and one booth. Upon entering the little town of Tecate, simply follow the signs marked "San Diego" with arrows. From the time you enter Tecate and exit the border is usually no more than a 10-minute time span. Weekends and Mondays can be more congested as this route is becoming more popular. This border crossing is closed from midnight until 6 am, and closing times can be periodically changed, so observe operating hours when crossing. Approximately 2 miles after crossing the border you will approach a left turn onto U.S. Highway 94. You will be west of Campo and 38 miles east of San Diego. This route is a bit longer overall in time and distance but you will not have to pay any tolls and the border wait is shorter and less taxing. Also, you will enjoy some beautiful country scenery and not encounter a traffic stop until you reach Tecate. See our map section for illustrations of this text.

*Travel tip: When traveling on the toll road, stay in the extreme right hand side of the right lane when not passing another vehicle. The cause of many accidents is slower vehicles being sideswiped or rear ended by passing vehicles traveling at high speeds.

Legal Issues

The Method of Offshore Yacht Transfer of Ownership and Proof of Time Spent at the 90 Day Yacht Club

Perhaps the most confusing and misunderstood facet of the whole 90 Day Yacht Club experience is the actual means of physically performing the transfer of ownership and then proving the whole process was successfully done to the California tax collector. We will now explain, to the best of our understanding, how this is done. The whole nebulous process is not spelled out in plain English by government decree so we will describe the currently accepted method, that has satisfied the taxman in many previous instances to date.

Not many years ago, you were required to follow your new boat in a chase boat and physically be transferred at sea from boat to boat outside the 3-mile limit of the State of California's jurisdiction. Following that rather adventurous event, particularly if the weather wasn't calm and cooperative, you were to exchange the purchase check and transfer documents and then disembark the now previous owner on the chase boat and take your boat immediately out of the area north or south to another State or Country. All this action was to be chronicled on film and witnessed on paper for later scrutiny by officials of the State.

We were actually involved with one of these deliveries in the mid-70's, when a newly constructed Defever powerboat was launched and put out to sea. We had spent 3 months in a San Diego boat yard installing and wiring all the electronics on the yacht and went along for the ride when the delivery was performed. It was a harrowing experience to say the least. It was a dark December night and a storm had just left the area leaving the seas sloppy, putting the difficulty level up to a factor of 8 on a scale of 10.

> ### State Board of Equalization Tax Law
> ### Title 18, Regulation 1620
>
> Property delivered outside of California to a purchaser known by the retailer to be a resident of California is regarded as having been purchased for use in this state unless a statement in writing, signed by the purchaser or the purchaser's authorized representative, that the property was purchased for use at a designated point or points outside this state is retained by the vendor.
>
> Notwithstanding the filing of such a statement, property purchased outside of California which is brought into California is regarded as having being purchased for use in this state if the first functional use of the property is in California. For the purposes of this regulation, "functional use" means use for the purposes for which the property was designed. When the property is first functionally used outside of California, the property will nevertheless be presumed to have been purchased for use in the state if it is brought into California within 90 days after its purchase, unless the property is used, stored, or both used and stored outside of California one-half or more of the time during the six-month period immediately following its entry into this state. Prior out-of-state use not exceeding 90 days from the date of purchase to the date of entry into California is of a temporary nature and is not proof of an intent that the property was purchased for use elsewhere. Prior out-of-state use in excess of 90 days from the date of purchase to the date of entry into California, exclusive of any time of shipment to California, or time storage for shipment to California, will be accepted as proof of an intent that the property was not purchased for use in California.

Now outside the 3 mile limit, we maneuvered aside and jumped onboard, timing our jump just right to avoid taking a swim. Having never sea-trialed the boat with the owner, I needed to go aboard and check out some new systems with him after the transfer took place. These tasks successfully complete, we left the owner and his wife to take the boat all the way to Coos Bay, Oregon, on their first long passage aboard their new yacht. I am happy to report all went well and many happy years were spent cruising the boat from Mexico to Alaska, as well as a trans-Pacific trip to Hawaii.

Currently the law is less stringent, as after you take offshore delivery you are allowed to come back to your California port and spend what time is necessary to ready the boat and yourself for leaving the State for the prescribed 91 day period. Notice we wrote _91 days_, not 90. The 90 Day Yacht Club is a bit of a misnomer; you will owe taxes if you do not spend a full 90 days plus one day offshore.

You must, however, leave the State within 89 days of the transfer of ownership, as we now understand the law is being enforced. But, we ask, why wait and tempt trouble by testing the 89 days statute? A tax assessor may interpret this rule differently at a later date. He may deem a lesser amount of time appropriate by the time your case is reviewed.

You may now ride the new boat out with the old owner and simply do an exchange at sea and return to port with the same crew. Due to liability factors the chase boat method of transfer of parties involved has been discontinued as the accepted delivery process. You may want to chronicle the whole delivery on film. Be sure all the pictures have the date inscribed on each negative by the camera. This photo taking record at one time was an important part of the process, but now we understand the photos to be of a lesser value to the tax officials.

After your position is verified by GPS as being outside the 3 mile limit you may commence the performance of exchange of money, ship's papers, and the resultant hand shake. At this time all parties involved in the offshore delivery process must sign an Affidavit of Delivery with the latitude and longitude of the transfer recorded. The broker should have all the paperwork on file for the transfer of ownership.

An often overlooked aspect of the transfer is the insurance of your new yacht at the time of the sale. You should have a cell phone onboard to facilitate a call to your insurance broker to provide an insurance binder _after_ the transfer is completed. The date and time on the binder will be viewed later as a critical proof of when the transfer of ownership at sea ocurred. Be aware also that the new owner may not pay for the slip fees at either the California or Mexican marinas or have any work performed on the boat until after the offshore delivery is completed.

Now we have the term "functional use" within the law as a guiding hand in the next phase of the delivery. The new owner may not navigate or use the boat in any way until the delivery has been performed. After the exchange of ownership has been performed the new owner must use the boat as intended at sea during the initial cruise. If you are on a sailboat, raise the sails and enjoy an ocean sail on your new yacht. If you are on a fishing boat, throw out a few lines and try to catch dinner. If you are on a party boat, well, party!

At this time the transfer of ownership of the vessel has been officially completed and you can start to enjoy one of the two happiest days of a boat owner's life. This being the day you bought the boat, and of course, the other day, in the far off future, the day you sell the boat. So now, you and the previous boat owner can sit down together at the helm and share the happiness of your two similarly satisfying, but at either end of the spectrum, days. This being done, the trip to your new port in Mexico can begin or you can head back into your California port to ready the boat for its trip south.

If you are buying a new boat, this exchange will be made with your broker in the same manner. We don't advise skirting the actual method of transfer prescribed as it could mean you fail to satisfy the terms of the current law, and could possibly be made to pay the tax at a later date. While most brokers are knowledgeable in the general aspects of the offshore delivery process, please remember they are not tax professionals. You may want to consult a maritime tax attorney that is licensed to practice in the State of California regarding the delivery process that is being accepted at the time of sale. Whatever plan you decide to employ, congratulations are in order as you have now completed the first phase of your enrollment in the 90 Day Yacht Club.

You are now ready to travel to your port of destination in Mexico. One of the benefits of waiting to travel south for a few weeks after transfer is that you will have your new boat's documentation of ownership in hand in your name and the proper proof of insurance, also in your name. You may want to add or upgrade your new boat's equipment before the trip with some of your soon to be realized tax savings dollars.

After making all of the necessary preparations and you feel that you are ready to depart, we advise you to take the drive along the coast to Ensenada and familiarize yourself with the landmarks and topography of the route you will be taking south by sea. While in Mexico, you can make reservations at your marina and intended destination point of entry into the country. Bring your ship's papers and proof of boat insurance, in case it is asked for, and be sure these items are back on board the boat when the boat arrives in Mexico.

As your new yacht disembarks its California port and arrives at its Mexican port, take more dated photos. Collect and save all the receipts for fuel or other services performed on your date(s) of departure and arrival. You are now entering the receipt-collecting phase of your time spent offshore. Pay for everything with your credit cards when possible, saving your receipts at the time of transaction and your statements at the end of each month. Save all of your paper work upon checking into the country, both from the Port Captain and the marina office that checks you in. Ask for and save receipts for every dollar spent while in Mexico.

One of the nice features of using Marina Coral for receipt collection is that they can give you a computer printout of all your transactions made while at the marina. Check-in charges, monthly rent payments, diving services, phone calls, charges made at the restaurant and pool to your slip number. All these will be kept as a record of your time spent at the 90 Day Yacht Club. When you are ready to leave, a full accounting of your time spent has been recorded and will be printed out for you in the marina office.

Now we come to another somewhat non-descript area regarding the law. The term within the law is "functional use" and the fulfilment of that use of the boat is very important. We see new owners leave their boats at the marina and not return for the entire 91 day period and then the boat disappears back to the States and that's all there is to their fun of being in Mexico. No cocktail parties, no bar-be-que parties, no stops at the fuel dock after a day spent out cruising the bay, no days by the pool, and no trips into town for dinner or to the market. And most importantly, these boaters have nothing to show as proof that the boat was used while offshore.

These people are in complete non-compliance with the law regarding offshore delivery and not having to paying their tax burden. Bringing a boat to Mexico as a _tax avoidance_, rather than as a _tax compliance_, are two different intents. The boat, while in an offshore state of existence should be used extensively to satisfy the spirit of the law. Actually, the true and righteous proper fulfillment of the law's intent and implementation would have you visiting and using your new boat weekly while offshore.

Within twelve months after the date that you purchased your boat, you will receive a bill for the correct percentage of the reported amount you paid. No getting around it, you will receive a bill. Everyone, whether they did an offshore delivery or not, receives a tax bill for the amount of sale. At this time you will be asked to pay the bill in full to avoid any future interest accrued if your claim for the exemption is denied. As a past member of the 90 Day Yacht Club, you will claim the offshore delivery boat exemption, under the mutual understanding between you and the taxman that you complied with all the rules in the delivery process and used the boat while it was offshore. This is done by completing the form BOE-106, which states why you are claiming the exemption and is then signed and dated and submitted with the proof of your yacht's offshore state of existence.

In order to prove your compliance, a trip to your favorite copy shop is your next stop. But first, do you remember the position of your offshore delivery as reported by your GPS and recorded on the Affidavit of Delivery? Locate that spot and illustrate it on a chart and bring that along with you to the copy shop. Copy every receipt you have, the Affidavit of Delivery, the chart position of the transfer, and the insurance binder at time of delivery in groups of however many you can get on each page copied. Keep the originals of the paperwork in a safe place if needed for further verification of your tax status in the future. If you have copies of your delivery photos, you can send them along in an envelope. Once you have a stack of pages of copies, including copies of the computer readout from Marina Coral that you may have, have them all spiral bound and, viola! You now have the 7%+ of the purchase price of your not so new anymore boat in your hands in book form. Staple the envelope of photos on the inside of the back cover to complete the job. Mail all this to the tax officials, and if you did everything properly you may hear nothing more from the tax office. The fact that you complied with the law and earned the exemption will not be acknowledged by the taxing agency. A call to the tax office at least one month from the date you filed your proof may render an answer as to if you qualified.

Please be aware that the methods prescribed and recognized by the State Board of Equalization continue to change as the employment of the law evolves from year to year. Your yacht brokerage firm may have an attorney they can suggest you contact to discuss the proper fulfillment of this offshore delivery process.

We wrote this book in part to show you how to do the actual offshore delivery process, and also to help you feel comfortable when traveling to and from the boat in order to be in compliance with the law. You will find your time spent in Mexico to be memorable and will look forward to your next trip south. You will also welcome your next boat purchase as an opportunity to again spend time on your new boat at the 90 Day Yacht Club in this beautiful country.

Navigation South

Waypoints and Landmarks

Leaving or returning to San Diego Bay, we choose to use San Diego Harbor Bouy 5 as way-point 1 at coordinates 32 39.132N and 117 13.636W. If you are joining our sail plan from north of San Diego, you will be using the next waypoint at Punta Descanso as your first Mexican ter-ritory waypoint when traveling south. Two maps in our map section illustrate your passage south.

From Bouy 5 to waypoint 2 is a distance of 24.3 miles at a course of 153 degrees magnetic. This will find you abeam of Punta Descanso at a position of 32 15.504N and 117 06.457W. At approx-imately 32 31.N and 117 11.W you will be crossing the demarcation between the United States and Mexico. To starboard you will be approaching the Coronado Islands and to port you will observe the bullring on the bluff just south of the low lying river bed, where the border line runs from Tijuana to the sea. During this passage, take care when abeam of the large smokestack on the beach at Rosarito Beach. When approaching this area you will observe an array of large mooring bouys along your course. These are connected to the oil refinery on the beach by underwater pipelines and should be passed on the offshore side (the Coronado Islands side). There are often one or two large tankers moored to these bouys. Also, be watchful for an assortment of small craft in this area. The coordinates 32 21.150N and 117 05.748W are at this vicinity of increased activity. At Punta Descanso you will see a large high rise building just south of Popotla where the movie Titanic was filmed. A large crane marks the Fox Studios lot and a collection of movie set buildings.

You will now steer to waypoint 3, Punta Salsipuedes, at 31 59.983N and 116 54.040W. This will be a distance of 18.7 miles at a course of 133 degrees magnetic. This leg of the trip will find you the farthest offshore, more than 6 miles between your position and the town of Puerto Nuevo. Between, you will see Sugarloaf Rock, a small brown and white moving object against the shoreline backdrop. Above the Puerto Nuevo area, on the hills, you will see graded dirt roads, as yet only serving a few houses spaced at various places on the hill.

Rounding Punta Salsipuedes you will discover a group of large pink and yellow buildings on the tall bluff. You are now en-route to Punta San Miguel at 31 53. 531N and 116 46.038W, a distance of 9.3 miles while steering a course of 121 degrees magnetic. This is the most desolate passage of the trip, reminding us of days gone by when pirate sorties raided the Manilla galleons which carried rich-es along this coast to the east during the Gold Rush. Or perhaps the hills of southern California dur-ing the early 20th century, undeveloped and as yet unspoiled by over population and scarred by tract home projects. Steep mountains rise abruptly from the sea, a remarkable contrast of topography and a sight of awe-inspiring beauty. You are now starting to savor your first glimpse of the isolated and pri-mal lands which are the mesas, arroyos, deserts, and sierras of Baja California. As recently as the 1950's, the whole of Baja was served by only rutted dirt roads south of Tijuana along the entire route to La Paz and Cabo San Lucas.

As you round Punta San Miguel, you will be entering the large bay of Todos Santos. To star-board are the two closely grouped Todos Santos Islands, and to port is the shoreline leading to Ensenada. Across the bay is magnificent Punta Banda, your gateway south for further adventure. Your next waypoint, and last of the trip, is 1/2 mile south of Punta Morro and the Marina Coral. You will now steer an approaching course of 102 degrees magnetic and 5.3 miles later you will arrive at 31 51.276N and 116 40.285W. En route, you will pass a rock jetty enclosure, home to the local commercial fishing boats adjacent to the El Sauzal fish processing plant. Also, you will see large round white petrol tanks on the hill just northwest of Marina Coral and Punta Morro. As you approach Punta Morro, you will begin to see a jetty with sailboat masts visible around the point and above the rocks. You should stay at least 1/2 mile seaward (south) of the point and jetty as you pass to the southeast corner of the marina where you will find a small entry facing east. See our Marina Coral map which illustrates the marina layout and approach.

If you choose to continue on to Ensenada, the entrance bouy at the end of the east (shore side) Ensenada entrance jetty has coordinates of 31 50.403N and 116 37.582W. Be aware the charts in this area are inaccurate and night and foggy approaches are not advised without radar and careful depth soundings. See our chart inaccuracy map that illustrates the amount of error that can be encountered on the charts of this area.

We hope you will experience a safe and an enjoyable trip en route to your stay as a member of the 90 Day Yacht Club. When returning north, simply reverse the waypoint order, and subtract 180 degrees from the bearings to reverse your course going to your Stateside marina home.

Bon voyage !

Trip Preparation and Implementation

Readying the Boat for the Trip

One helpful aspect of your trip to the 90 Day Yacht Club is that you have just had a survey of the boat completed as a part of the sales process. This information concerning the condition of your new boat is a valuable tool when evaluating her seaworthiness during the trip planning phase. Any repairs to the basic systems that propel and keep the boat afloat should be performed before departure.

Emergency gear must be in place and in working order as well as navigation resources and electronic navigation aids. Charts of the area you will be traveling are a basic ingredient for your safety, and a working VHF radio and depth sounder are essential. A GPS and radar are handy if you encounter fog or bad weather, which may cause poor visibility. An autopilot, while not required, serves to make the passage more enjoyable and leisurely. An EPIRB is not a vital piece of gear to have aboard, as you will always be in sight of land and will probably have a cell phone aboard if you need assistance. A vessel assist card is a good investment for the first year that you own the boat, until you are familiar with the boat and are sure of her condition. The structural quality of your boat outweighs the size of your boat when evaluating seaworthiness.

You will be navigating in the open ocean and you should be aware of the possibility of encountering all possible weather conditions and be prepared for an unexpected breakdown of an onboard system. If the boat you bought sat at the slip unused for a long period of time, the condition of the fuel must be evaluated. Once at sea, wave action can cause the accumulated dirt at the bottom of the fuel tanks to well up and clog your engine's fuel filters. Carry spare fuel filters as well as spare pump impellers. We suggest new impellers be installed in all pumps before departure or at the very least, be inspected. A coolant and oil change should also be performed before getting underway.

These suggested pre-trip procedures are inexpensive insurance against finding yourself adrift and having to deplete your Visa card balance for rescue and repair costs. Preventive maintenance when preparing and operating a boat is the key ingredient that will decide whether your day spent out on the ocean is one of delight or despair.

Boat Licenses and Documentation

When entering Mexico you must have proof of vessel ownership and port of registry. This can be a U.S. documentation certificate, a bill of sale, or ship's papers from the State which holds the boats' registration. You must also present proof of boat insurance when entering most Mexican marinas. This can be either of the two forms of insurance discussed in the following section. If you plan to do any fishing or are carrying fishing gear or dive gear, you must have a Mexican fishing license for the boat and for every person aboard. Failure to do so would risk you having to pay a large fine and possible seizure of your boat. Simply having the gear aboard without the proper licensing is a violation. You needn't be fishing to be breaking the law. If you don't plan to fish, leave the gear at home and visit the Ensenada fish market. It's by far cheaper and safer! Also, if you plan to operate a Ham or Single Side band radio in Mexico, you must have a Mexican radio license.

Insurance in Mexico

When traveling by boat in Mexico, it is best to have two forms of boat insurance. The standard policy that you would ordinarily carry in the U.S. is your first line of protection. This is necessary to present at most yacht marinas before they will allow you admittance to a slip. This policy usually contains liability and replacement insurance and should be carried at all times whether at sea or during happy hour at the dock. It would cover the clean up if your boat should sink at the dock, a fall taken aboard by a guest, or fix any damage incurred or inflicted in the event of a collision with another boat or the land. Some policies in the U.S. require a surcharge if you are operating the boat in a foreign country. Consult your agent as to whether you need this additional coverage.

The other insurance you will want to consider is a policy written for Mexican liability. If you happen to damage another boat and/or hurt personnel aboard the boat, this insurance is indispensable. Without this insurance you will be liable for a cash settlement and may also face imprisonment. You can find an agency that deals with Mexican liability insurance in either Mexico or the U.S..

Captain and Crew

Before heading south, an evaluation of the skills of yourself and crew as to seaworthiness and competency is suggested. If you feel you do not have adequate experience to make the trip securely, consider hiring a skipper or enlisting a friend to make the passage a pleasant and relaxing experience, complete with safe arrival at your destination in Mexico. En route, you will gain an invaluable education as to the handling of your new boat and an insight into the performance of a properly navigated passage.

Before leaving the dock, a review of the boat's emergency gear, onboard operating systems, and running gear should be performed with the delivery crew and Captain. A contingency plan to handle emergency situations, such as a man overboard, should be discussed. A pecking order of responsibility, a watch standing schedule, and half hourly engine and bilge inspection procedures should be reviewed. Once safely celebrating your arrival in Mexico, a debriefing on the merits of the crew's performance is recommended at Hussong's Cantina over a beverage of your choice.

All passengers and crew onboard must have personal identification for the check-in procedure at your Mexican port of arrival. Before departure, have all parties on the boat check to be sure they have their ID. The best form of ID is a Passport, but a driver's license is accepted. We understand a birth certificate with a notarized letter of authenticity is also acceptable, but the two forms of photo ID mentioned above are universally accepted, and will not cause you any unnecessary extra explaining or delay while completing this already time consuming process. For a small fee, most Mexican marinas will do the check-in process for you, but you will still need to present ID for all of those arriving in the country with you on your boat.

Checking Into Mexico

We advise you to let the marina you are entering in Mexico do the clearing in and out paper work for you when you arrive and depart. This can be done for a nominal fee and will be well worth the small amount of money spent. But if you choose to do the procedure yourself, be prepared to make trips throughout town from the Immigration Office, to the bank, and to the Port Captain's Office with copies of crew list, crew tourist visas and crew identification in hand. Interpretation of the procedural rules vary greatly from port to port and you should consult your broker, local marine store's publications, or the office that documented your vessel before departing for Mexico to obtain the most recent information.

If you plan to have your boat in Mexico for more than 6 months, you should obtain a 20 Year importation document when you initially enter the country. We can remember when Mexican law stated that foreign boats had to leave the country every six months. This permit will allow you to cruise Mexico for 20 years without leaving the country. Many boat owners are under the misconception that this document allows unlimited importation of new gear, spare and repair parts into Mexico for the boat, duty free. This is far from the truth and many boaters have found that out the hard way. While some customs officials recognize this permit for importation of boat supplies, many do not and the rules applied are subject to the interpretation of the official you are dealing with at the time of importation.

When dealing with Mexican officials, two ingredients will make the process run smoothly and expediently. A good attitude is essential, regardless of the sometimes stressful situations which may surround you. A smile and a few Spanish phrases will help oil the works! Regardless of how good or bad your Spanish speaking attempts may be, the mere fact that you made the attempt is the important factor. Also, when you arrive at the office, your clothing is the first impression that will be evaluated by governing officials. Be aware they have seen it all, from hippies to hotshots, and you are entering their country as a guest and should dress respectfully. Barefoot and barely clothed is OK in the marina, but in town you are in an entirely different environment, governed by a Catholic mentality, so dress accordingly.

Guns and Drugs in Mexico

Possession of firearms or drugs will find you in a Mexican jail. Do not get yourself in the position of having to hide or jettison these items if stopped and searched by Mexican Officials. It's simply not worth the risk and/or consequences, and the Mexican judicial system cannot be as easily manipulated as we are accustom to in the U.S..

Marina Coral and Hotel

Fuel

There is only one fuel pier in the Ensenada area and it is located within the Marina Coral Basin. Both diesel and gasoline are available. Due to demand, the fuel supplies may run dry. It's best to contact the marina on VHF Channel 71 first to confirm availability. Fuel can be had in the Ensenada harbor but must be trucked in by drum to your location and hand pumped aboard.

Facilities

As a marina guest you are at equal status to those in the hotel. Catered meals can be ordered at the slip and complete banquet rooms can be reserved for large functions. There are 3 pools, including one shallow for children with submerged lounge recliners and one indoor. There are 3 Jacuzzis, one outside and two inside. You will find pool tables, ping-pong tables, table hockey, and volleyball and tennis courts. A gym in the indoor pool area offers a steam room, sauna, private showers, massages, and towels for the pool and shower areas. The hotel bar and restaurant offer a great view of Bahia Todos Santos. There is a large fish cleaning area, but if you prefer, you can call the marina and have your fish cleaned by marina personnel. You have free cable TV on the docks but you must supply your own cable line. Bagged ice can be ordered at the marina office. There is a launch ramp, pump out service, bottom cleaning crew, and boat washing personnel. Laundry machines are adjacent to a grassy picnic area. The water on the docks is not recommended for drinking. Bottled water can be ordered for delivery to the marina. Entry and exit papers can be processed by the marina office for a nominal fee. Security guards roam the docks 24/7 and entry to the hotel and marina is guard and gate controlled. Contact the marina on VHF Channel 71 for any needs you may have at your slip.

A full service marina store is located in the marina dockmaster building. Supplies you have forgotten or need may be found here. Mechanical repair by store personnel is available 24/7. Fishing licenses can be purchased and processed at the marina store. Helpfull referrals to downtown service locations are available; such as canvas repair, refrigeration, and woodworking.

Climate

Ensenada weather is much like that of southern California. Summers are rarely hot as strong afternoon west to NW winds directly from the ocean keep extremes of temperatures rare. Winters are milder with less windy days, but winds can sometimes be stronger than summer winds, fueled by storms from the north. A healthy surge can be experienced at Marina Coral and the Ensenada harbor docks. Therefore, extra dock lines are advisable; spring lines at both beams and double lines at both bow and stern cleats. Chafing gear should be in place at all wear points.

When traveling north, night passage is advisable after the daily 15 to 25 knot winds subside.

Southerly passages can be made during the day as you are traveling downwind. Any passage should only be attempted after consulting local radio weather forecasts and weatherfax if available. The Internet is also a valuable source of weather information.

Keep in mind that a sailboat traveling at a speed of 5 to 6 knots will require 12 to 15 hours to complete the passage, so weather planning is essential. A powerboat that planes at 25 knots can do a 3-hour passage in the early morning calm-no problem!

We have heard complaints of, "When does it ever get warm?" in the summer, and seen heavy iron pool furniture blown into the pool during the winter. Other winter days can be so clear and warm that the Marina Coral pool beckons you during morning coffee. We've experienced days so humid and sticky that the pool calls you 24 hours a day for a number of days, as summer hurricanes from the south dissipate during their northerly journey. Bahia Todos Santos is located directly on the Pacific Ocean, therefore there are no geographic barriers to protect the area from the always changeable weather patterns associated with an ocean climate. Regardless of the weather, you will delight in the lack of smog, absence of constant air traffic (a passing plane is a noteworthy event), and the feeling of being surrounded by a vital, natural and healthy environment.

	Below is the average temperature and rainfall per month.											
	Jan	Feb	March	April	May	June	July	Aug	Sept	Oct	Nov	Dec
Temp	54	55	59	59	63	64	68	70	68	63	61	60
Rain	3	3	1	1	.3	0	0	0	0	.8	.8	3

Temperatures in degrees F and rain measured in inches.

Flag Protocol

When entering Mexico you must have two flags flying. This is customary as a courtesy to the country you are entering and recognized by international law. The placement of these flags is not important, but an American Stars & Stripes and the Mexican green, white, and red must be displayed. They should be approximately the same size as having a huge U.S. flag and small Mexican flag is considered bad etiquette. Once settled in Marina Coral these flags may be stowed away. Marina Coral is like a little country, separated by the excellent security and secluded location. If you are docked in the main port of Ensenada, it is recommended that you fly both flags. This is because there is more authority and activity in the port. All trips away from the dock from both locations should be accompanied by a display of both flags.

You may not want to leave your flags hauled because they have a tendency to discolor and eventually shred in the elements. Today we had a visitor ask why some Mexican flags are green, white, and red, while others are blue, white, and red. Dependent on the quality of the ink and cost of the flag, the green fades to blue on some flags. Flags hoisted high flying in the breeze create a festive atmosphere when viewed from neighboring boats, so keep flying them if you can afford to keep buying them!

While You Are There

Telephones and Cell Phones

As recently as 10 years ago a telephone connection in Mexico was a difficult commodity. The most popular local bars had a phone for the benefit of the whole community but the line of folks waiting to use it could be long and background noise a problem. Now there exists a newly installed series of cell phone towers from the border to Ensenada which can be seen by the side of the toll road. We have found the use of Baja Cellular to be the best means of local communication in the Ensenada area. Calls from the U.S. can be costly, one dollar a minute is typically the norm. But local calls are only 20 cents or so per minute. The Baja Cellular system is another phone number assigned to your phone and the time is prepaid. A phone number can be called to keep track of the time remaining on your account, quoted in Spanish and in pesos. You must have a phone capable of storing your stateside cell number and your Baja cell number as well. Of course, you could keep it simple and choose to pay the cost of roaming to your stateside server.

You can buy Ladatel cards in various denominations at various downtown locations that allow you to use prepaid service at Ladatel phones located just about everywhere. There are also long distance phones located in some pharmacies that allow pay per use at the time of use at booths located in the stores. All in all, phone availability is no problem in our new technological age. And the sound of brass bands and screaming alcoholic celebrants need not be the accompaniment to your call to your broker or church social worker.

Taxis, Trains, Trolleys & Buses

A very simple and inexpensive means of personal transfer aside from driving your own car from points north to Ensenada exists. For the return trip the reverse method is employed. An Amtrak train can be taken from Los Angeles or San Francisco to the main downtown San Diego train station. There you can transfer to the trolley to San Ysidro and the border for a cost of under $5. Then walk across the border to a large bus station 2 blocks from the border that has bus departures direct to Ensenada. It is the building with a large white sign reading "Terminal De Autobuses" mounted across the top front of the building. You can't quite see the sign or building as you cross the border, so bear to your right toward the tall mirrored buildings with a pink "Medac Central Medico" sign mounted at it's top. The bus station is just beyond that building. If you need to ask directions to the bus station, everyone seems to speak a little English at the border. Do not let a taxi guy slam you in his taxi for another more distant bus station. The bus to Ensenada currently costs less then $10 and the driver will drop you off at Marina Coral if you ask him en route. That will save you the cost of a taxi back from the downtown Ensenada bus station.

If you need transportation in the Ensenada area, taxis are everywhere and the cost is seemingly arbitrary to the driver. From Marina Coral to Ensenada is a brisk 2-kilometer walk or a $5 to $10 taxi ride. Those with an adventurous spirit can find the little white and yellow buses stopping every 5 to 10 minutes in front of Marina Coral and for 70 cents you can take this southbound bus and travel to it's most southerly point of destination in downtown Ensenada. For an additional 70 cents you can take another southbound bus to its most distant stop at a rural community approximately 10 miles out of town, up a dirt road to the top of a hill and back to the downtown bus station. Another 70 cents at that point will return you to the marina. Our first week without a car at the 90 Day Yacht Club was spent exploring the Ensenada area on these little buses.

Pharmacies, Bakeries, and Banks

In the city of Ensenada you will find one of these three establishments on just about every street. The pharmacies (farmacias in Spanish) are well stocked with many items you would see in your local U.S. pharmacy. The big difference is that many items that you would need a prescription to buy in the U.S. do not require one in Mexico. We have stocked our boat with an emergency first aid kit, which contains painkillers, and antibiotics that would cost more and would require a trip to the doctor for written authorization to buy. Diet pills, mood relaxers, sex experience enhancers, and anti-sea sickness remedies can be found, and can be cross-referenced in the store's reference books as to the name and dosage. These stores often contain copier services as well as long distance phone service, on a pay per use basis. Many are open 24 hours and provide free delivery.

Bakeries (panaderias in Spanish) are seemingly everywhere. Often you will also find a bakery in the larger grocery stores. Every kind of perfection can be found from croissants to cakes. Usually you will see a stack of large round silver trays, along with a selection of tongs. Simply fill the tray using the tongs to collect the baked goods. We enjoy the coconut macaroons, baked fresh daily, as are all the goods offered. The La Baguette store is our favorite for fresh warm baguettes that remind us of our French campaigns, surfing the shores of Biarritz.

Banks (banco in Spanish) are found in all areas of central downtown Ensenada. Usually you will find banks busy and crowded and best to be avoided. For the most part, it is recommended that you use your credit cards and U.S. dollars for purchases, therefore avoiding the need to visit the banks. Your credit card statements and receipts are valuable when proving your expenses and activity in your foreign port. We do not find the time spent exchanging dollars for pesos to be time well spent. Everyone takes dollars, from stores vendors, to the beggars on the street. You should contact your credit card company and be sure they do not charge a surcharge for foreign exchange purchases. If you do need to visit the bank, perhaps the ATM machine will satisfy your needs most quickly. Otherwise you usually take a number like at Baskin Robbins or stand in a line waiting to be served. We advise you do both and take advantage of whichever happens first. The exchange rate is usually posted as to the buy and sell rates. When clearing in or out of the port, a visit to the bank is usually necessary to pay for port fees or for a Mexican visa card. Customarily, only one bank in town performs this service and gives you a receipt to show port authorities before you can be cleared. We advise letting your marina check you in and out. The small amount of money charged is well worth your time spent on your boat and not in the bank or the Immigration and the Port Captain's Offices.

Stateside Radio Reception in Ensenada

It is a characteristic of the FM frequency band that FM stations are very clear at short range but fade quickly when confronted with topographical barriers or distances over 75 miles. Ensenada does not receive any but the strongest U.S. FM stations and only when atmospheric skip conditions are good.

On the other commercial radio band, AM frequencies travel quite well over long distances. We rely on Los Angeles 1070 AM station KNX for 24-hour news and weather reports, which we can survey from a distance while sitting in the tranquility of our cockpit. Interestingly, this station can be received into the Sea of Cortez and is a good source of information on weather conditions coming from the north. When the Santa Ana winds are blowing in Southern California, it's a good bet the dreaded Northerlys are raging in the Sea of Cortez. San Diego 600 AM station KOGO is an all talk Rush Limbaugh type format with San Diego Padre baseball games and Art Bell at late night which provides border traffic reports 24 hours a day, 7 days a week. San Diego 690 AM station is a 24 hour sports talk station and perhaps the strongest station due to their transmitter tower being on a hill near Tijuana. Many FM and AM stations in Ensenada feature U.S. oldies and some current music releases. Various major sporting events such as the World Series and the Super Bowl can be found on the local non-cable Ensenada television channels and you can listen to the commentary on U.S. AM radio stations in English.

Road Fuel

The operative word here is Pemex. This is the abbreviation for Petróleos Mexicanos. The only gas stations you will find in Mexico are going to be Pemex, easily distinguished by the large green signs. This national oil company is responsible for everything from exploration to pumping the gas in your car. Gas is sold for cash, credit cards are not accepted.

There are usually two kinds of gas; Nova in blue tanks that contains lead, and Magna Sin, in green pumps which does not. Gasoline seems to have an octane rating of around 86, so expect a lot of pinging. A higher lead free fuel is available near the border which is better than Magna Sin, but more expensive. Diesel is carried at most stations, which contains a high sulfer content, making changing your oil more often advisable if you use a lot of Mexican diesel fuel.

We usually avoid buying gas in Mexico, as the cost is often more and the fuel quality questionable. There is also the issue of exchange variable from station to station. The rumor is the independently owned stations franchised by Pemex give you a lower amount of value for your dollars than the stations directly owned by Pemex. The large station as you enter Ensenada just after crossing the bridge has always been friendly to us and never presented a problem. We have felt less then well served at the station in the center of El Sauzal.

The fuel is sold in quantity by the liter. One gallon is 3.78 liters so multiply the cost of a liter by 4 and you will have the approximate cost per gallon. You will find that all stations carry fuel at the same price. When arriving at the stations look for a sign posting the exchange rate or ask the attendant for the rate that day. All of these stations are full service and tipping is not necessary.

Ensenada Entertainment

In the town of Ensenada you can find plenty of diversionary endeavors. Videos can be rented usually in English with Spanish subtitles. Movie theaters offer first run movies in the original English release with Spanish subtitles. Most of these air-conditioned theaters offer movies for under US $5. If you need to satisfy your Internet habit or e-mail the folks back home, Internet café's abound in every corner of the city. Just three years ago, there was only a few prominent Internet cafés in Ensenada, and now there are many in all areas of downtown. If dance is what you desire; disco, techno, jazz, classic rock are all to be found. Yes, also there are floorshows designed for the entertainment of men, as in all other major cities on the planet. Strolling minstrels, more commonly known locally as mariachis, can be hired to sing your favorite Mexican songs on the streets or in the many cantinas and restaurants. A trip to the main beach south of town will be made more exciting if explored by a spirited horse. Helicopter tour rides, harbor cruises, and road trips to see the Punta Banda blo-hole (La Bufadora) are all popular forms of entertainment enjoyed by both tourists and Ensenadans. Just hopping one of the little yellow and white buses that passes every 5 to 10 minutes at Marina Coral will take you to the extreme south edge of town and back. Walking along the waterfront of the harbor is a popular pastime for the locals and a stop for ice cream at the Darigold Stand along the way is suggested. Weekends find the local car cruisers cruising, the open-air theaters filled with song and karaoke, and the horse drawn carriages full of tourists. Stores offering a variety of goods and trinkets line the Ave. Lopez Mateos. At night, families gather to enjoy firework displays sold in Ensenada stores. Hot Springs are within an hour of town in the mountains complete with changing facilities, bars and restaurants. If the Circus is in town, do not miss it, as a Mexican traveling Circus is a special treat.

So much for thinking that all there is to do is to watch TV on the boat at night. Ensenada is a thriving little city and should be enjoyed to its fullest extent.

Traveling Around Town

On our site map and in our site map index we refer to " the 3 heads street" and the "flag pole street". This tradition of using landmarks to establish your location in Ensenada is largely due to the fact that the street signs in town are practically non-existent. Outside the 8 block tourist area, it seems as though the budget for replacing missing street signs ran dry in the 1930's after the U.S. repeal of Prohibition brought an end to that boom-town era. Ensenada street maps can be found in our map section.

After realizing the geometrically-square street layout exists, one expects to travel down a street until seeing the appropriate sign for the destination's street address, and turn in the proper direction, and find the numbered endpoint to your quest. But we have found ourselves lost in new areas of town and thrust into the blind limbo of a "where are we?" mode. Can you count to 10?

No, we don't refer to 10 counting as anger management. It's an easy way to orient yourself when traveling away from the harbor area where these 3 heads and the flagpole reside. The touristy shopping street is Ave. Lopez Mateos, aka. and street #1. Continuing away from the harbor to the northeast is an easy 2, 3, 4, and viola! - Ave. Juarez, which is #5. After that, you are on your own, as to how high you can count, or when town ends - whichever comes first. But above all, keep counting or you'll lose track and have to retreat to your last known position (quote Dorothy, "There's no place like home, there's no place like home"...).

The other direction, the 90-degree angle of travel, is a bit more challenging because actual names are employed to seemingly keep you confused. Is this why those three past Mexican dignitaries heads are preserved for their valor and a monolithic flagpole has been erected in a phallic display of Mexican national machismo? Really, did the head statues and pole come first, or the desire to know where you are in town? Guess we'll never really know... But we can visualize a couple of school children calculating the time of day, day of the year, inclination of the sun, and the position of the flag pole to help them get home from school!

In this direction, it really is helpful to have a map in hand. No, there's no alphabetizing of names for cheaters, and a semblance of order does not exist. You are thrown an interesting array of names, on non-existent signs that if asked for relevance in a game show setting would have you buzzed or gonged in a heartbeat. It's an interesting note that all Mexican towns use the same names to entertain their visitors, but not necessarily in the same order! While not wanting to insult our Mexican hosts or reveal our ignorance, we ask respectfully, isn't there a Washington, Franklin or Maple in your history, or a Mexican jail that makes street signs?

Now those statues and the flag pole landmarks come in handy. Simply look down the streets toward the harbor and orient your position by number of streets traveled from the last sighted statue or pole waypoint. If you someday graduate to be a sage and savvy True Traveler of "uptown" locations and memorized points of centralization, you can consider yourself a bonified "direction giver".

In between the streets, numbering is straightforward, progressively higher as you travel further up the block. Between 2nd and 3rd streets we see specifically random selected numbers in between 201 to 299. Between named streets we see the same trend from 0 to 100 each block.

Don't expect to find that your right-of-way street will continue that way for it's entire length. You may encounter many varied methods of traffic management on one street from block to block. This is especially important to note, as you or another car from the opposite direction may assume wrong and run a stop sign at a 4-way stop, or a two way stop. Always drive for the other guy in anticipation of his (or her) mistake! And always, please, in a foreign country, stop for any and all pedestrians and nod and wave them on with a smile and a mutual respect. You are the visitor and should act accordingly.

Back to the game show reference, *WILDCARD!* When have you ever sat in the middle of the street and observed two posted business addresses on each side of the street with different street names? Well, this may be an intriguing diversion from the reality of your day found in some areas of Ensenada. While researching street names for our maps, we were treated to two names for many two-lane blacktopped paths. Obviously, they didn't move two inches and warrant a new tape cutting celebration. We surmise another entity with more money and/or political influence caused the divorce in name, or the co-habitation. Be forewarned, fellow True Traveler, you may see two names on one street within a few blocks! If you do find yourself entirely lost and confused, drive back down to the ever looming flag pole, and enjoy a walk along the waterfront and relish in the fact that you were only confronting the "little stuff" of life.

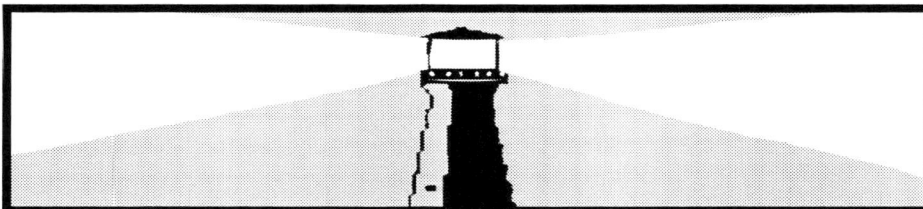

Shopping

Ensenada has no indigenous crafts to speak of, most of the products offered for sale come from the interior of Mexico. The atmosphere is less intense than in Tijuana, where a hawking jumble of hustlers are encountered at every turn. The mood is more sedate in Ensenada.

Experienced True Travelers know that Ensenada is perhaps the best city along the Baja to shop. The stock of goods is abundant and the prices are lower than at the border towns, yet still offer a margin that permits a friendly bargaining dialog. After all, no one really pays the asking price in Mexico, a country renown for its enjoyment of spirited negotiation over the final sale amount.

Most of the daily cruise ship tourist dollars are scattered among the many shops lining both sides of Ave. Lopez Mateos and within a 1-block area on each of the side streets. The main shopping zone extends from Ave. Ruiz to the Arroyo de Ensenada. Pottery, woven fabric blankets and serapes, colorful embroidered dresses, onyx figurines and knock-offs of major brand sunglasses are just some of the products offered. Cuban cigar stores are becoming more numerous but we suspect many cigars offered for sale to be questionable as to their actual origin. A thriving fireworks cache operates, a typical 4th of July celebration is an incredibly expensive display of burning powder all the way around the Bahia Todos Santos.

The sad faces of the tiny Indian children from mainland Mexico will tug at your heart, begging with their paper cups. Unlike the truly poverty stricken children you see in Tijuana, these children are a part of a scam. This is their job, however young they may be. The unseen facet of they're seemingly meager existence is that they live on communes in groups outside Ensenada overseen by male patriarch's. These women and children are trucked to town every day and pimped along the boulevard in a staged display of poverty, when in fact, the men hiding in the shadows unseen, collecting the benefits of the daily take, are only using them. Truth be told, we imagine these men live a far better standard of life than their conscripts, left daily in the hot sun to play a pathetic role. But when you are not looking, and the prospect of a tourist dropping a peso or two their way is exhausted, they can be observed smiling and enjoying each others company.

If you are evaluating the purchase of a new trinket made of what is represented as silver, be aware that the vendors in the tourist zone insisting their wares are authentic silver may be stretching the truth. Mexican law requires manufactures to stamp a number of either ". 925" (the percentage of silver in sterling), or ". 950" and ". 999" (pure silver) into each piece of silver, with the signature mark of the manufacturer of the jewelry. Non-existent or unreadable marking indicates the product may be made of alpaca, an alloy of copper, zinc and nickel, and not containing any silver.

Along the boulevard you will pass a Hussong's logo clothing shop that appears to be linked to the bar and it's popularity over the years. You would expect this to be an appendage of the bar and the family that has owned and operated the establishment. Well, it seems someone else saw the monetary wisdom of marketing gear with the name posted on the bar displayed proudly by tourists wearing Hussong's clothing returning to the States. A trademark legal battle ensued and the clothing shop is actually operated by ownership connected only to the bar by name, and not by family association.

The Ensenada area is known for it's fine wines. A stop at one of the larger Gigante markets is advised if a larger selection of wine is desired. The pricing is economical for both wine and hard spirits. Mexican Bacardi rums, an array of tequilas, and a selection of other non-domestic liquors are available at all markets and liquor stores. The large markets generally have more favorable prices and containers of greater volumes. The sale of alcohol is prohibited before 10 am each day and on national and local election days.

If you are staying at Marina Coral, there is a store in the Hotel that offers the daily San Diego Union Tribune (at a higher price to cover importation and shipping costs). There is also a rack with many current U.S. magazine publications and books. A stock of products which you may have forgotten, such as suntan lotion, is available. A selection of Marina Coral logo clothing is offered to commemorate your stay at the Marina or Hotel, or to supply you a replacement for those sweatpants you left at home in the U.S.

We lost that black light velvet Elvis painting we bought in Mexico in a co-habitation dispute many years ago. And the onyx chess set we had stored for 40 years was recently sold at the swap meet. A remembrance of a set of bongos painted with palm trees purchased by our parents when we were children warms our hearts. But one of the most precious of all the possessions we have during our time spent at the 90 Day Yacht Club is the night spent at anchor in a quiet cove at the Todos Santos Islands devoid of any noise or light except for the sound of lapping wavelets on our hull and the light in our eyes in appreciation for the experience shared. Not all of our most special Mexican belongings are store-bought on the Ave. Lopez Mateos.

Food, Water Availability and Quality

We have now been in Ensenada for 4 years and are happy to report that the dreaded diarrhea bug has never befallen us. We enjoy all of the foods sold in the markets, using the common sense precautions, washing vegetables thoroughly and keeping foods refrigerated and sealed in zip lock bags. We eat at restaurants with total trust, sometimes avoiding coffee and iced drinks to protect ourselves from unnecessary exposure to questionable water.

Water has always been a source of problems when in Mexico. We have all heard the cliché warning, "Mexico is a great place to visit but don't drink the water". Truth is, the locals buy all their water as they too know the tap water is contaminated and unhealthy. Many trucks are seen delivering 5 gallon bottles of water but if you have your own 5 gallon container, purified water stores and machines are everywhere selling water in bulk form at a better bargain. Water can also be found for sale at all the liquor stores and markets in smaller quantities.

If you are at a restaurant and desire a glass of water or a coffee, the tradition is to ask if the water is purified. We speak a little Spanish, enough to get by. Simply asking "Tienen ustedes agua purificada?" will illicit a simple yes or no response. The major tourist eateries do not want to risk bad publicity within tourism circles by making their patrons sick and generally have purified water. We are never shy to ask at all restaurants regardless of how fancy they are. Ice is chancy, as its origin may be tap water. Hopefully the liquor mixed in with that margarita will kill whatever bug is in the ice. Drinking iced refreshments at small out of the way bars has been the source of many a tourist's long night spent visiting the bathroom repeatedly. The most effective remedy can be found at any farmacia. It is a little box of tiny white pills called Lomotil. Like magic, this medication works wonders and is an over the counter product.

We have an icemaker on our boat and in order to keep the ice from contamination we must have clean water supplied to the line that automatically supplies water to the icemaker. We could call the Marina Coral office and have bottled water delivered by truck in 5-gallon containers and poured into our tanks. This is an option you may want to consider while at the 90 Day Yacht Club. Instead, we have installed "The Water Fixer", which you can find in many marine supply catalogues. This device has two filters, an initial large mesh pre-filter and then a very fine mesh secondary carbon fiter. The water is pumped through these filters and then channeled into a stainless steel tube that encloses a florescent germicidal lamp. Whatever bug makes it through the filtering process is zapped in the lamp chamber. This allows us to use the water straight from the dock supply. This clever little unit, costing under US $500 has paid for itself many times over.

The produce found in the local markets is amazingly abundant and the diversity of selection wonderful. There is no railroad connecting Ensenada to the North, so products found in the stores are either trucked in or shipped in by container ship. The surrounding valleys are fertile with agricultural rancheros sending their yields to the hungry, growing Ensenada populace. Pricing is reasonable, an avocado selling for US $2 in the States can be bought for 2 or 3 to the dollar in Ensenada, dependent on their size. Toasted avocado, bacon and cheese sandwiches seasoned with Spike (found at your local U.S. health food store) on baguettes, with Sabritas chips are one of our favorite Ensenada treats.

Meats are fresh cut daily and the supply again is found to be more than adequate to keep your bar-be-que busy. Beef is not traditionally aged as in the States so you may notice a little difference in taste. No problem for a good chef with a little imagination and seasoning to correct! Try a sprinkling of sunflower seeds and a dash of Worcestershire sauce in your next bar-be-que bacon sirloin cut cheese-burger to spice up the mood. The prices are again really a bargain. A nice t-bone or New York steak can be bought for 2/3'rds of Stateside pricing.

Four of the main staples of local life are rice, beans, chicken, and tortillas. They are cheap, fresh, and found everywhere. Many poor families eat these four foods in varied forms of recipes nightly, with beef meals mixed in occasionally when funds are available. Bar-be-que breasts of chicken, sprinkled with Creole blackening seasoning, in bean, rice, and cheese quesadillas are also one of our favorites meals.

And then there are the bakery goods; breads, cakes, fruit turnovers, croissants, French-style baguettes, etc. are all baked fresh daily. A stop at a Mexican bakery is a special treat. For a few dollars you can fill a brown paper bag full of your favorite confections. The rewards for that long day of toil are often found being gathered on the big round trays at your local panaderia by Ensenada madres of the casa. The crispy on the edges, chewy coconut macaroons are our favorite choice for added calories.

Perhaps the best is left for last. The time and fuel spent to get that super-yacht fishing machine out to the banks and back could have been saved by a quick trip to the waterfront fish market. Pricing is very reasonable and the supply is unbelievable. The chicken of the sea label comes to mind but that would do an injustice to the flavor of perfectly bar-be-qued albacore or swordfish.

Our advantage, living here in the marina, is the fishermen withdrawing from that fish-kill lust, quickly get tired of cleaning the 40 or so fish they just scooped from Mother ocean, and are usually good for a long fillet and occasionally a whole fish! It's not uncommon to see a dock cart full of 20 or so fins, sticking straight up, being wheeled to the fish cleaning area.

By the way, the diabolical practice of cleaning fish in the marina and tossing the carcasses is forbidden by marina policy and considered bad marina etiquette. It not only attracts the seagulls, which leave deposits that harden like concrete on the neighboring boats. But a few days later, after the fishermen have returned to their Stateside jobs, the stench of those beauties rises to the surface reminding us of a bad B-movie horror flick we have experienced in real life, "The Curse of the Floating Dead Fish".

Speaking of seagulls, if it were legal to eliminate these pests with a pellet gun as many of us wish we could, and they tasted like chicken, we would all enjoy many free bird bar-be-que meals!

Traveling home and freezing these freshly caught piscatory platters is a strange ritual, a fresh fish should remain just that, so the full flavor can be savored. But if you want one of those fish as dinner in the off-season month of December for a Christmas family fish surprise, we can understand the concept. We fashion a foil pan to contain a melted combination of butter and Lowry's seasoning salt or Creole blackening seasoning over the bar-be-que grill, and cook those golden gills 'till they're white, dry and flaky, and a little bit charred on the edges. Cubed-cut potatoes in the microwave with a little water become mashed cheese potatoes to compliment the festivity. Mix in a salad with mil isles (thousand islands) dressing and, viola!, culinary ecstasy on the high seas! Gracious señor Jesus!

 OR

???

Personal Experiences

Tijuana Tequila Tiempos

The 60's were great years to be young and emerging. Those times were truly special and I enjoy sharing a gratification for the gift of creation during that era. We had many conveniences previous generations did not enjoy that are often taken for granted: electricity, running water, a greater life expectancy, the mechanized age, worldwide communication and travel, and color TV. We saw the evolution of records to 8-track tapes, to cassettes, and now to cd's and dvd's. During the Summer of Love, while listening to music from the Quicksilver Messenger Service, Grateful Dead, Jefferson Airplane, Janis Joplin, Jimi Hendrix, the Steve Miller Band and the Doors; a new oneness of being was being realized and shared. Timothy Leary was encouraging all to tune in, turn on, and drop out. Drug experience was worn like a badge; the trips were in your mind and not on a highway. Donavon sang of e-lec-trick-a-banana, inferring that banana peels would get you high, and telling us they called him Mellow Yellow.

I also enjoy sharing my appreciation of the fact that I was born in perhaps the most perfect of all areas of the world and in the finest city of that area-San Diego. No humidity or bugs, mild temperatures year 'round, and 20 miles from a country of bars that allows you to drink at the age of 18!

1965 to 1967 were my high school years and we did a bit of scuffling around Ave. Revolution in Tijuana. We explored the dark and dangerous side streets where a real or imagined tales of Donkey Shows and Spanish Flies (don't ask) was proliferated. This was just after the early 60's reign of a young musician who rose out of the streets of Tijuana to be discovered by the nation in a movie named Woodstock, to be known during his professional career as Carlos Santana. He played in the same bars we were then carousing and leaving at the first light of day. A typical night started at the Hotel Nelson for quiet warm-up cocktails, the Long Bar for rowdy beers, and then to Mike's Bar for a dance 'till dawn attempt to score a girl. The song "Brick House" brought everybody onto the floor, "Light My Fire" was sung with a heavy Mexican accent and space up front next to the band was a premium.

The famous Long Bar (now gone), was one of those loud bright-lights bars made famous by what else, it's long bar. This was Tijuana's Hussong's Cantina equivalent; mariachi bands, beer by the huge pitcher full, arm wrestling, and camaraderie with total strangers speaking little of your language, or you speaking little of theirs. If you met American girls here, they were usually game to spend the rest of the night with you and your buddies dancing in another bar.

At the close of the night, we'd pile in the car and drive back up to San Diego occasionally taking a little extra time to make a side trip. Instead of continuing back up I-5, we'd drive through Imperial Beach to the Silver Strand and to the now defunct Coronado Car Ferry. For a couple a bucks a car, the little ferryboat would transport us quietly across the bay to what is now Seaport Village.

One of these nights in TJ we were with a buddy that was intent on scoring an ounce of hippy lettuce from somebody on the street. Regardless of our attempts to dissuade him due to the danger of being arrested, dealing with an unknown element, and the "take it back across the border factor", he was still ready to lay down 10$ to a stranger for a bit of loco weed. Soon he was happily striding back to us, hiding paranoid in the shadows, proclaiming he had met someone who was soon to hook up with him and complete the deal. One could find mood altering uppers or downers in the farmacia easily bought over the counter. This nefarious means of dealing was a bit scary and new to us. Was our friend dealing with an undercover policeman, or worse, a criminal that may use an act of violence in an effort to rip him off for the 10$? That was big money in those days.

What happened next was the realization of another one of those classic common stories told by those who'd spent time in Mexico. Our buddy went and did his deal and nonchalantly we removed ourselves from the area before examining the newly purchase "stash". It was truly a righteous amount he said, but he had not examined the contents due to how many people were on the scene at the time of the exchange. We finally reached a quiet back street area with a bit of overhead light and opened the paper bag to discover the zip lock bag inside indeed was as big as reported. Upon opening the zip lock bag, a whiff of the contents confirmed the fact that this was truly an exotic blend, but was a bit different in fragrance than what we expected. Passed around to all, we finally agreed, yes, this was an extremely rare form of mind-altering substance-oregano! You know, the mint seasoning Origanum vulgare... We had a good laugh over that one, after the shock wore off, and told our friend he had better stick to smoking banana peels. Forever, after that day, we called him Mellow Yellow.

Puerto Nuevo, the Lobster Town

As young surfers en route to our favorite surf spot, San Miguel near Ensenada in the late 60's, we often found ourselves at Km 38 instead, at one time an undeveloped bluff where we camped and surfed a perfect kelp protected right point break. I'm reminded of one long, cold winter night on that desolate point. It was just myself and my high school surfing buddy Barry, camped out with bedrolls, surfboards, tortillas and cheese, and a few cervezas. Out of this black night emerges a Mexican Federally (police officer). Known to be less than honest dealing with gringos during that frontier era, we were less than elated to greet this uniformed pirate. After paying him a few hard earned dollars for him to allow us to camp out at this deserted, barren location, he just as quickly disappeared into the night.

Just down the two-lane paved road Highway 1 at Km 44 was a fishing community marked only by a huge 7-up bottle painted on the side of a building. We'd drive down a dirt rutted and dusty road to a little row of restaurants as classic as the waves we'd ripped all day developing a huge appetite for cervazes and some comida delicioso. We were soon treated to the legendary Newport meal; grilled lobster, refried beans, rice, homemade tortillas, butter, salsa, and limes to squeeze into our cold Coronas and Pacificos. Of course, everything was cheaper then (gas was .28 a gallon, but we still had to scrounge contributions by all to make the trip), and this meal was a true value as the restaurant prices were geared to the level of the local community.

Today you will find a full-blown town with full-blown prices to match. The tourist dollar and the new venture attitude by establishment owners have caused the price to be multiplied by a factor of 5. And the main road into town has been paved! The weekends are busy and wild with gringos and strolling brass bands and you often have to park on adjacent dirt parking lots. An artisan market lines the entrance to restaurant row: items including pottery, serapes and blankets, t-shirts, jewelry and other local fare can be purchased. The overwhelming fragrance of the cooking food may have you hurrying by these goods in an attempt to get seated and fed. No worries, these trinkets will be waiting for you to buy and lug up to the States after dinner, perhaps later wondering why you bought that black light velvet Elvis painting, or the painting of little dogs playing poker at the table that displays all the vices known to man. The tambourine with the two balls suspended on strings and the wood cup with the ball on a string are two of our favorites.

Although, once only a pleasant stop during the drive to Ensenada or for a one-day tripper, many hotels have opened in the area. This has made Puerto Nuevo a self-contained destination where you can dance on the tables 24 hours a day until the bewitching hour, when you are obligated to return to the States and attend to your day job and otherwise normal lifestyle. By the way, that once quiet, desolate bluff at Km 38 is still there, but now is unrecognizable due to "progress", and the influx of the tourism dollar so needed to improve the standard of living of this still poor and once remote area.

Speeding in Rosarito 1967

While driving though the town of Rosarito, hurried, hot and frenzied for waves south near Ensenada, we were subjected to a lesson in the Mexican judicial system. We had just stopped for our favorite treat, fresh hot corn tortillas with homemade Mexican cheese. We would simply make a quick rolled taco with chunks of cheese and the semi-melted squeezed delight would make our lives complete! We now can find the same experience at the Tortilleria Rentaria which you will find on our downtown Ensenada site locator map.

Now we were back on the road in hot pursuit of liquid refreshment, waves, and not really paying attention to our speed. I glanced in my rearview mirror and discovered a police car following closely. What the guy in the passenger seat was doing attracted my attention. It was a young guy in an oversized Mexican police hat performing an act that is etched in my brain as truly classic. His head and hat were hunched into the lower right hand corner of the front window glass with his one finger-extended, fisted left hand rhythmically pointing across the length of his face into the corner of the window, to the roadside curb, at the pace of a flashing light. The universal sign to pullover!

This dutifully understood, I made my way to the side of the road and was told I was a speeder and to follow these guys a block to the police station. Upon parking and approaching the little one room building, we noticed a group of people sitting out front. We were told to wait outside and the conversation with these other "offenders" revealed they too were speed lawbreakers. How much I asked, and why are you still here? Their reply was they were waiting for some money to be wired to them from the States to cover a 200$ fine. My surf chum Barry and I had about 35$ cash, tortillas and cheese, 2 surfboards, our clothes, some beer in the car, and the car, no more.

Next we were called into the station to receive our destiny from the Chief officer of the city. Realizing at that moment that I appreciated the two years of Spanish I was forced to take as pre-requisite to graduating high school, I conjured up a tactical offense. My operative strategy was to use the approach-behavior begets behavior. As mentioned earlier, attitude is key when dealing with authority in Mexico. In my most remorseful and understanding fashion, mixed with some measured smiling friendliness, I stammered in pig-Spanish that I understood that many children play in town. "Lo siento", or in Spanish, I am sorry, and we would be careful to not speed ever again. Mix in a little "la familia esta bien?" (is your family well) and "quantos ninos y ninas tienes usted?" (how many children do you have?), and I felt the atmosphere start to warm a bit.

A bit more conversation with the Chief and all the money we had except a little bit I talked them into leaving us for gas, and we were walking out the front door with our newly found friend, the Chief, past the group waiting for a money wire. During the initial stop and search and after being finger pointed to the side of road, the original two cops found some beer in our cooler. We usually bought Mexican beer south of the border but for this trip we had brought down some U.S. domestic. Thank God for that, because as we left the station, the Chief put his arm around me and asked in perfect, but highly Spanish accented English, "You guys got any of that good Coors beer"? His officers must have told him what we had, and it seems in fining us and releasing us he had figured in taking all our beer... Coors... his favorite.

Well, that left us with some gas money, tortillas and cheese, our boards, our clothes and the car. We managed to stretch all that into a weekend of perfect surf at San Miguel near Ensenada and I had a story to tell you in this book 35 years later.

Broken Boat in Ensenada

I'd worked in San Diego repairing and installing electronics since 1974, and in December 1978 I signed onto a 50 foot Alaskan powerboat with my friend Mike, to travel the yacht to Central America. It would be the owner, Mike and myself, on a luxurious top-dollar ride to banana land. The owner would at times not be present and we would have the yacht and it's amenities to ourselves. Needless to say, things didn't go as planned. But, as usual, I was smiled upon, and was shown the way to my next adventure in grand style. As the Mexicans say, one door never closes but another opens.

As fate would have it, we burned out the starboard transmission near Isla San Martin, some 95 miles south of Ensenada. We limped back to Ensenada on one leg and tied up at the commercial wharf. In those days there was only the commercial docks, the sport fishing docks, or the anchorage area in the bay. There was no Baja Naval, as that area was a huge area for Naval parades and the docks were as yet non-existent. The first night in town, my two companions took local transportation to the border in search of a replacement transmission and a little time to spend with their family after such a long arduous trip of one day.

That night was a night from hell for me as a winter storm blew into Ensenada that evening and kept me busy until morning light. The wind was gusting on the nose of this expensively appointed beauty, and as we were only side-tied in a stone walled corner of the no frills tuna seiner zone, the perfectly varnished transom and swim step were in jeopardy of demolition. I attached fenders aft, exerted leg pressure and generally had a miserable 8 hours of timing my defensive tactics against the gusting wind and pouring winter rain. A neighbor even tried to put out our bow anchor on his skiff as I applied weigh with the one good engine, but to no avail as the bottom was composed of soft mud.

Morning came and the damage was minimal. The guys returned that day to say the parts were on order in San Diego and they'd be back in a few days and we'd motor the boat back to San Diego for repair. Meanwhile, we took the boat out to a safer refuge and anchored in the little harbor of Ensenada. Did I mention why they were going back home for a few days? Christmas...yes me, in a foreign port, and on a freaking broke down luxury floating hotel, alone, on Christmas Eve.

No worries, I had money, a real neat place to sleep, and one cassette tape. I bet I can still sing you every word on Al Stewart's album, "Time Passages" (and how they have).

The only way to get into town from the boat was a call on the VHF to Juanito's sport fishing boat taxis or a wave of the hand to the kids operating the pangas from the anchorage to shore. I saw a familiar face motoring by that evening and hailed him to give me passage to shore adelante, er, pronto. I had befriended this kid and given him a tour of the yacht after one of my trips to town previously and knew he slept in his panga pulled up on shore at the now site of the Baja Naval docks. That would prove to come in handy later that morning.

I arrived at the shores of Ensenada on Christmas Eve and paid the kid a few pesos and told him to expect me in a few hours for the return trip. My destination, Hussong's Cantina for a bit of Christmas cheer. You know how it is to enter an empty bar and think that maybe you've entered a time warp and that it's actually after closing, and the barkeep is sweeping the floor in preparation for the next day? This probably happens annually at Hussong's Cantina, reflecting the rich tradition of more than a century of good times gone by in pictures on the Cantina walls. Those ghosts of Margaritas past come out every cold winter Christmas Eve night to occupy the bar stools and stupor once again.

At the bar sat one lone patron, a Loren Bacal style beauty, advanced in years, resplendent in a dress endemic to the local region. I half expected her to look at me and say "you do know how to whistle, don't you Steve? You just put your lips together and blow"...

I sat next to her, bought her a glass of wine and learned that she was an expatriate from the States and had just returned from California with a load of presents for the orphanage due to be delivered tomorrow on Christmas day. Suddenly my woes paled in comparison to the light in her eyes. I was in the presence of an angel! The most poignant moment of our encounter was when she got up to leave the bar and her cane (which I hadn't noticed) fell into the area inside the foot bar and I picked it up, gave it to her, and without a word we nodded a sign of mutual respect, and she hobbled out into the night.

I was ready for a bit of frivolity at this moment and I wheeled around to survey the scene and lo and behold, there were now three American girls sitting at a table, alone, in a slightly more uplifting setting than the suddenly self-imposed melancholy I now felt. I approached the table in full swagger mode, filled with the knowledge that women like guys that have boats (even though it wasn't my own). Also, they were in a rather remote circumstance, and I needed to raise my spirits... A few rounds later and the one of the three I liked the best, suggested we drive the other two girls back to San Diego in order for them to celebrate Christmas with their families. Well, we drove those other two girls back to San Diego, dropped them off in seemingly opposite ends of town and drove all the way back to Ensenada in the wee hours of Christmas morning.

We parked the car and hurried down to the panga I knew was my secret stash for a quick trip back to my now newly realized floating Hugh Hefner remote retreat. It's now 5 am and the little guy is crashed out completely. I shake him and he doesn't wake. Being aside a female with all the right motivations, and an oh so intuitive grasp of the "moment', she shakes the guy in the most private of areas, he wakes up with the cutest smile and is ready to answer the call to duty.

Two days later my newfound female friend heads back to San Diego, the guys arrive for the journey north to San Diego, and the spell is broken. All the while "Time Passages" marked the moments spent on this, another Mexican adventure.

Marina Etiquette

This is being written after being, yet again, awakened by the surge of two high power diesels being started at high RMP's, spewing noxious smoke and toxic fumage into our hatches, filling the boat with a new atmosphere lingering long into the morning, due to it's heavier than air blend of airborne oil and carbon monoxide. Not quite what I had in mind as a compliment to my coffee, and far more bracing as a wakeup call. Some weekend mornings, when the 90 Day Clubbers are here for their frantic two-day collection of receipts, and the sport fishers are vying to be the first on the banks to boast, we are reminded of the Indy 500, after that cute little old lady says "Drivers, start your engines". The difference is, this is a race that starts at 3 or so in the morning and keeps starting all day long.

This is obviously an uncontrollable and inevitable element of marina life. We'd have to be at anchor somewhere every weekend to avoid the carnage. But there are witnessed many other instances of a just plain arrogant, in your face, attitude. Or sometimes it's simple absentminded ignorance. Like that precious little scruffy dog, a few slips down, that seems to bark at that certain piercing volume and pitch all day long. And the owner's, John and Martha, are oblivious to the din, having lived with this somewhere in Placencia their whole lives. When we complain, and the dog is put down below, peace is restored again, until next weekend when the process starts all over again.

We have a couple that has lived aboard at Marina Coral for 4 years. These folks enjoy piling their stuff in one of the marina dock carts, and sit there at happy hour and relish the glory of having a personal charge at the wait. While the rest of us walk the length of the marina looking for a cart, realizing the time spent finding, or not finding one, could have been spent making the 5 trips required to carry all our stuff down to our boat. We sigh, boil it down to "needing the exercise", and carry on realizing all that unpleasant karma those cart hoarders are creating.

Then there was the guy who wouldn't buy the electrical cord splitter to supply shore voltage to both banks of his AC panel. Why, pray tell, are boats wired that way anyway. So, of course, this new boat owner needed to start his generator at 6 in the morning to heat the boat and run his stove. And his genset exhaust was right at our bunk hatch! Incredibly, no amount of "suggestion" would dissuade him from this behavior, nor would he buy the proper cord. Luckily he was only here a few weekends, and finally left the marina one morning, without checking out of the country, and I might ad... with more bad Karma.

The slip next to us has contained a plethora of novice "yachters". Like the "captain" of the brand-new 45 foot sailboat that insisted on practicing docking with his son, with no line handlers on the dock. We shared a space without a dock finger between us, and he was upwind of me. One fine, sunny, windy day he was in full docking procedure mode, yelling out orders in the most authoritative of tones. Lines rigged to perfection, son in the proper strategic placement, and, of course, to raise the level of difficulty, backing in, into a stiff afternoon 15-knot wind. His tone changed to a wimpy "I'm in trouble" as he looked at me shortly before the impact. Luckily my davits suspend a fine natural fender, my 8 foot Carib inflatable, and the only damage was done to this "mariner's" ego. Karma?

One Friday night, at 10 pm, the engines in the powerboat next to me roared to life at the usual

20K RPM that it must take to insure these engines keep mechanics in business. Unlucky for me, the wind was such that all the fumes were settling on my deck and snaking into my hatches. I closed the boat tight and uttered a few unrepeatable words of welcome in the direction of the new boat owners next door in full "throttle-up" mode. I'd been through this routine before and waited for the time to pass until either their wrists got tired manipulating the controls or they ran out of fuel.

This guy's son had been down a few times before, installing a rad stereo dude, etc., and had told me they owned a "yacht commissioning business" in a condescending tone. Judging from the fish on the hook painted on the transom, in the motif of "kindergarten sketched with a 5 color waterpaint box", I doubted the validity of this claim. Very nice, a very primal contribution to this 200 thousand dollar boat.

Forty-five minutes later I heard a lady down the dock yelling "are you guys gonna run that boat all night long!" Well, bless her heart, she had raised the issue, so I took this opportunity to pile on. I took a deep breath of fresh air from the cabin and prepared to open my companionway door. Rather than just yelling "incoming!", I explained that they were pouring smoke into my boat and to get busy and shut 'em down. Well, these two "yacht commissioners" informed me that they couldn't shut 'em down! I explained the air and fuel starvation theory of arresting mechanical detonation, or maybe they should just pull the stop cable connected to the injection pump. That boat ran for more than 2 hours until after midnight, with these two thumbing through engine manuals with a flashlight until a marina mechanic could be summoned from home to turn the key off. The only help I could, or would, have rendered to these novice boat owners was a bucket of sand to pound up their... or should I say, into their air intake. A true karmic moment...

Then there is the current most fashionable of fads, next only to the ownership of an SUV and cell phone: choking, er, smoking a cigar. Reminds us of all the ye-hoos in the early 80's we saw attending San Diego Charger football games on TV when we lived in Seattle. Fresh off a mechanical bull, and chewing on a hayseed, were 55,000 spur wearing fadits knocking off each other's cowboy hats in response to a completed Dan Fouts pass. Truly noteworthy was that now forgotten urban cowboy era.

Smoking a cigar wouldn't be such a noticeable event if it weren't flaunted with the usual absurd flourish of seemingly understood importance, wealth and stature. The little cough in between puffs is a comical completion to the Renaissance man painting hanging on the wall of this guy's mind's parlor wall. And of course, each flick of the ash goes into our precious mother ocean's mouth. And when done carefully rolling that burning rope around in between those yellow fingers with little finger extended, without a thought, in the drink it goes, now resembling that floating tootsie roll in that old Bill Murray movie. The ocean is not an ashtray or a trash can-would you like it if we dumped all that refuse you uncaringly toss overboard into the ocean into your SUV, making it impossible for you to find your cell phone somewhere heard ringing in the big wet pile which surges out of the door in a gush onto your new suit as you open the driver's side door? Need we again utter the "K" word?

Finally we have the case of the bright red and white Nordhaven pinball. Marina Coral has rather narrow channels between docks and an entertaining weekend endeavor is a beer, some chips, and avocado dip, back dropped by new boat owner antics while docking. A wife falling off the bow a full 2 slips away from the assigned dock space and in the middle of the channel has been observed, failure to find reverse at 5 knots notated, and then there was the winner of the Golden Sombrero. During the tranquility of another quiet marina morning, one fine day occurred an event of truly noble scope. A brand new Nordhaven, which is built like a tugboat, pulls straight forward at an alarming pace and bow to bow powers into and mushrooms the bowsprit of the 45 foot power boat across the dock from me, driving it's swim step up onto the dock until the boats' dock lines stopped both boats' momentum.

The Nordhaven, now in reverse, releases it's grip on it's power boat dance partner and the swim step, now suspended in mid-air over the dock and a few feet from my boats' bow, settles down on the dock ripping out the step's mounting screws making an absolutely awful sound. The Nordy then backs down into the self-steering system of a sailboat. After the dust settles, this sweetheart of a guy has his insurance fix the damage on the powerboat because he was observed in that collision, but he denied contact with the sailboat, which was not witnessed, and refused to repair the now geometrically twisted self-steering mechanism. This left the sailboat owner to remove the assembly and cart it all up to San Francisco himself for repair.

As another man's karmic wheel spins into action, may the sun shine always on your hatches grasshopper... and we advise you to keep your insurance always current.

The Price is Right

Mexican TV can be very entertaining. Versions of many games shows can be found complete with the same set and format with the host waving arms at prizes speaking Spanish and mimicking Bob Barker. One evening I was channel surfing and found the Mexican version of the Price is Right. Contestants from the audience encouraged to "come on down" in Spanish, while jumping up and down and in and out of the host's arms.

As the show wound down to the big prize package segment, the curtain went up to unveil an old style VW bug, say maybe a 1973 vintage super-beetle. I didn't quite understand the Spanish commentary and commented to my friends that they were giving away a used car. Later we had a good laugh when we discovered the old style VW Beetle is still in production and sold new at local Mexican car dealers. They are one of the least expensive new cars available in Mexico. One mile from Marina Coral on Highway 1, you will find an agency that will provide you with a test drive and the chance to find out if the price is right on your new nostalgic VW bug.

Local Knowledge

Islas Los Coronados

The Pirates of the Coronado Islands

On increasingly rare days, they dominate the southern horizon from San Diego to La Jolla with their prominence. Other days they are completely hidden in the mist and smog. The Coronado Islands have long been the subject of conjecture and debate as to their true history. Steering a course of 171 magnetic from San Diego Bouy 5 will find you 14 miles later at the South Coronado Island north light. Legend has it, this was once the gate to a lair of cutthroat pirates that preyed upon ships traveling south from San Francisco.

Barren, rocky, and now only home to sea lions, sea birds, reptiles, a few goats, and lighthouse keepers; these islands were aptly named Las Islas Desiertas when discovered by Juan Rodriguez Cabrillo in September, 1542.

Historians write that in 1602 Sebastian Vizcaino named the Coronados in honor of Francisco Coronado, Governor of the province of Jalisco under Hernan Cortez. Onboard Vizcaino's ship were a group of Carmelite friars that are also reported to have named the islands Los Cuatro Coronados in November 1602, November 8th being the day of Cuatro Coronados, commemorating four brothers put to death for their Christian faith in the time of Diocletian. And to futher cloud the issue, a chart created by Vizcaino during his explorations names the island group San Martin, so the true origin of the present name is the subject of wide dispute.

Other names, due to the likeness of a coffin struck by one of the islands, have been associated with death. The Sarcophagi, or Dead Men's Islands nomenclature was used to solemnize this portrayal. Corpus Christi was the name of North Island for a period of time, it supposedly resembled a body draped with a shroud. North Island was also known as the mummy island, reminding observers of the contents of Egyptian tombs. Many a wary passing ship steered clear of this mysterious collection of dark foreboding shapes.

By the time the film crews arrived at South Coronado Island to make the first Mutiny on the Bounty movie (using the south island to duplicate Pitcairn Island), the Spanish name Los Isles Coronados had been settled as the officially recognized name.

The Legend: As the Gold Rush raged in Northern California, a band of bloodthirsty pirates flew the skull and crossbones on South Coronado Island and used a cave now known as Pirates Cave as their hideout. Ships traveling south from San Francisco carried rich cargos of newly mined gold to the East and their course lay directly abeam of the pirate's nest.

The leader of these thieves was Jose Alverez, his origin either a castoff from LaFitte's hearty lads banished from New Orleans or a deserter from the Mexican Army. Regardless of his true past, it is known that he stole a schooner from a Mexican port, and after arming it with plenty of cannon and saber wielding scallywags, he made his base on the Coronados. In a clever game of hide and seek, he set up business in pursuit of the buccaneer's goal of fortune and fame.

The fame factor was to elude these troops, as the barbarous practice of taking no prisoners and scuttling every vessel they assaulted made tracing their actions impossible. It was assumed by the shipping companies that the missing ships were the victims of foul weather or unseen shoals, and they were reported as lost at sea.

A vessel named the Chelsea was apprehended and as the passengers and crew were being killed, a cabin boy named Tom Bolter proclaimed, perhaps in earnest, or in the desire to save his bones from Davey Jones, that he had long admired Alverez and wished to prove himself a worthy addition to the cutlery compadres. This feigned or real adulation fed the ego of Alverez and in addition, the fact that young Tom knew the sailing dates of future shipments of riches, cajoled Alverez into breaking his vow of murdering all and he spared Tom his life. This breach in the pirate's take no prisoner's code would prove to be their undoing.

After two devastating raids of ships, tipped off due to Tom's information, the cabin boy considered himself now a pirate of great repute and questioned Alverez about the size of his share of the captured booty. An argument and fight ensued and Tom only escaped with his life due to the fact that he had information valuable to Alverez. You see, Tom had smartly only given enough information to make himself still useful if in the event he became expendable.

Tom was left in the cave under armed guard while the pirate ship embarked to plunder the next galleon to arrive from San Francisco, using Tom's information of the next ship's expected passage of the islands. The second day after his imprisoning, the guards lapsed in their assignment of duty, and Tom succeeded in freeing himself and killed them both.

He set sail in the pirate's fishing dory, loaded with as much treasure as she would hold, and soon arrived at the waterfront hide houses of San Diego harbor. His arrival prompted much attention from the sailors collected to greet his landing. He was invited to tell his story aboard the Boston vessel Grendo. His claims of buccaneering braggadocio brought exclamations of amusement and disbelief from the assembled sea dogs. They demanded proof in the form of captured riches and were all sobered by the display of loot Tom produced to back up his story.

The hide houses and whaling station on Point Loma were solicited for any volunteers wishing to form a raiding party to sail to the Coronados and rout the returning pirate brigade. An overwhelming response to the call saw a formidable force of San Diego wharf rats boarding the Grendo for the Islands. When they arrived, the Grendo was hidden behind the South Island with only a skeleton crew, the main body of the others stationed on the island out of sight in wait. Tom assumed his position as if he were still under guard in the cave, with a man to pose as guard.

Upon their return, the pirates dragged their plunder up the cliffs to the hideout, leaving their arms aboard the schooner. Taken completely by surprise, the struggle was soon over and the pirates, bound and beaten, were loaded onto the ships for the sail to San Diego and an appointment with the yardarms. As the lot were hanged, more than a few harsh words of condemnation were heard to be cast in Tom Bolter's direction.

The pirate schooner was sold, it's proceeds and the captured loot were divided amongst the men who had brought the criminals to justice. Tom demanded the largest share, making him a man of wealth and stature and to some a hero.

Tom Bolter's future was a dark and dreary one due to the stigma bestowed upon him by the ghosts of his betrayal, and he was soon the scourge of the waterfront clan. He became such an onerous presence, that many felt he should have been hanged with the rest. A day came when he disappeared. Some rumors had him fleeing to Mexico to escape the pirate curse, but no one missed him, nor did anyone care that he was gone.

Be careful not to venture too close to South Coronado Island, matey, as his ghost may be watching you through an old spyglass from Pirate Cave, evaluating your new treasures, as you travel south to the 90 Day Yacht Club...

Biggest Wave Bounty

The biggest wave ridden by a human was the subject of a bounty offered by a prominent surfing magazine in the early 1990's. The wave had to be in the Pacific Ocean and recorded on film. It was an incredible challenge that included the huge winter waves of the north shores of Hawaii, Northern California, and Australia. Surf spots like Waimea Bay and Kaena Point in Hawaii, Steamer Lane in the Santa Cruz area of California, and the dozens of wild spots in Australia were thought to be frontrunners in the competition.

These world-renowned spots are known to support rideable waves of more than 20 feet high every year. The keyword here is rideable, as many spots attract big waves, but few maintain the shape necessary to be successfully ridden by a surfboard. In the world of big wave riders, just a few spots are widely accepted as candidates for capturing the wave needed to make that one surfer King Kahuna of them all. The fame and fortune, with the resultant endorsement moneys from the surfing industry, were a great attraction to the potential winners of that year's competition. As the rumors flew around as to who actually was up-front in the running and where the best spots were for the winning, the surfing world buzzed with excitement. When the winter storms of the extreme north and south latitudes send huge swells over thousands of miles of ocean to break on a reef that is perfectly shaped to make the swells jump to twice their size, the word spreads quickly and surfers from all over the planet board either jets or their old jalopy cars to get to the scene.

A surprising winning wave at a surprising winning spot in a surprising area of the world, won the prize for that year's search for the perfect monster wave.

Back in the mid 60's the Windansea Surf Club located in La Jolla, San Diego, discovered a new surf destination. It was 90 miles south of La Jolla and required chartering a boat, as it was 9 miles offshore and only accessible by boat. This was a spot named Killers by the crew, as it was a crushing wave of over 15 feet, if the swell was big enough and from the right direction. Adjacent to the big Killers waves, were spots called Chicken's, Rarely's and the Boat Launch Lefts. These were much smaller and forgiving in strength and many of the less brave-hearted souls preferred to hang here.

The location of this surfing Mecca for big wave seekers is illustrated on our Todos Santos Islands map. Si señor, the largest photographed waves that year were to be had at a rocky reef in front the lighthouse of North Todos Santos Island named Killers. The size was subject to some debate whether you were from the Hawaiian Islands or from California. The Hawaiian Islanders called them a 20 foot Hawaiian-style wave, but the Californians definitely saw 25 to 30 footers. In the photos, if a man is 6 foot tall and you can fit more than 5 times his height by spreading your fingers to his size against the wave, then we would call that at least a 30 foot wave.

Killers can be seen breaking from the shoreline of Ensenada on the extreme north end of the Islands with the naked eye when it is "on". A horizontal column of white water foam extending around the point can be plainly seen on the days when it's "working". If you are visiting the 90 Day Yacht Club in the winter months and the waves are raging at Punta Morro, you may enjoy a cruise out to see some of the biggest waves in the world, at Killers, Todos Santos Islands, Baja California.

27 feet
24
KILLERS
REEF
TODOS 18
SANTOS
ISLANDS 12
6

The Construction Crew of Mexico

During our travels in Mexico, we have noticed a common feature of the panorama that defines the backdrop of your memorable 90 Day Yacht Club experience. In the most scenic and strategic areas of the hills and beachside communities you will see while cruising on your new yacht, or traveling through and visiting by car, there exists an alarming number of unfinished structures. Whether it is a villa on the seaside cliffs, a hacienda at the riverfront, or the estate by the lake, they are left to crumble as the local animal and rodent population lay claim to the empty multi-room, wind swept abodes. Did a pestilence suddenly interrupt the best-laid plans of men, did a bank foreclosure derail the progress of civilization, or did the cast of "The Night of the Living Dead" invade the labor force as the work was being performed?

We are talking about homes and multi-storied buildings that would be worth hundreds of thousands to millions of dollars if located in Southern California. With all due respect to our neighbors to the south, we have a playful theory that perhaps could alleviate the speculation.

A construction crew exists that is so far superior to all the others, that it is the only one called on to work on the many job sites available to be completed. They rotate throughout each Mexican territory when the priority list directs them to a specific location. The city of Ensenada completed a new bridge recently in one fell swoop that obviously had the funds and political pull to employ this band of talented artisans. Marina Coral had these craftsmen duly payrolled for the length of time needed to make the job complete. But just behind the marina there are empty high rise structures that were not so fortunate...

Whatever the *real* reason these unfinished projects are now blowing in the wind, we see a great opportunity for those who would invest in the possibility of their fortunes being tied to the many buena vistas viewed by these homes needing owners.

In the future, the narrowing bridge between our two bordering countries should make these unfinished projects more available to those wishing to own and occupy these properties and see them complete in their as yet unrealized potential beauty and refuge from the struggling toils of the over-populated California lifestyle. Enlightened generations from the north would be wise to find this short drive south a welcome relief, and an opportunity to forge a new self-realization of tranquility and the resultant renewal of spirit necessary for the survival of our race.

Your GPS and Chart Inaccuracy

We have included a map entitled "Chart #21021 GPS Position Inaccuracy" to make you aware of the fact that you, as captain and/or navigator, must be aware of the inaccuracies that may exist on any chart you use. In this instance, we happen to be using a Mexican chart for our illustration. Some of the charts available for your trip south to the 90 Day Yacht Club are truly vintage and should have been retired to the Nautical Museum and updated years ago.

From the 60's thru the 80's, an era of widely fluctuating Loran C signals, that were only reliable to about 60 miles south of the Mexican border, ruled navigation. The U.S. land-based Loran station's triangulation signals faded south of the border due to there being no existing Loran stations in Mexico. A mariner was usually on his (or her) own upon reaching the area of Punta Salsipuedes. In the early 90's, this gave way to the now taken for granted GPS era.

The first GPS we used was a little black box developed for the Desert Storm military operation by Trimble and was available for around $3000, if you could manage to find one on the black market. Prior to that we had to wait for a couple of hours for "a bird to come over the horizon" (a satellite) to give us a rough position on the widely used Magnavox Sat Nav (not really functional for a trip to Ensenada). Before that celestial piece of gear came along, it was the venerable land-based Loran C that enabled you to store that old sextant in the hanging locker.

We remember when a Loran C readout digit consisted of a vacuum tube that had all the numbers, 0 through 9, inside the tube illuminated by separate numerically shaped and stacked filaments, sequentially fired to show your position's numbers. These tubes were arranged in two rows, giving you readout of your position. If a number failed, you changed the tube. Your vessel was probably also being steered by a Wood Freemon autopilot and you had those classic mercury switch tubes stored with your Loran readout tubes. Those days saw you relying on a 1/2-mile or more accuracy, dependant on time of day, ionic atmospheric conditions, and your adeptness at re-initializing the Loran if it got lost. Dead reckoning your position was strongly recommended.

During the 80's, the government decided to spend a little cash for a "global positioning satellite" system, for military reasons. This led to what we have today, an umbrella of satellites that enable you to tap the resources of 8 to 12 "birds", for positioning, at any given moment, anywhere on the planet. Recently, the government discontinued its degradation of these signals. Due to security reasons, these signals from the satellites were scrambled to make your GPS receiver vary your position in an erratic, ever changing circle of extremes of more than 50 yards. In potential future times of a national threat to security, expect these signals to once again be degraded.

Today, the numbers you receive are good to within a few feet of your actual position and usually rock solid, and again, to a much lesser degree, dependent on atmospheric conditions. Another variable is the quality of your equipment. GPS receivers are designed to sample between 3 and 12 satellites for position resolution. You should buy a GPS unit that samples the most number of satellites, as this will increase your accuracy.

Many countries don't have the fleet of research vessels that are at the disposal of the U.S. government within the National Oceanic and Atmospheric Administration (NOAA) Corps, a branch of the

U.S. military. Having spent 2 years serving as an Electronic Technician aboard a NOAA ship, we know personally of the services rendered by these ships. Research of the positioning, and then charting of territories is one of their assigned duties. Tide survey, hydrographic (bottom) survey, and wild life survey are also performed. Unfortunately, a recent survey utilizing current charting techniques and GPS signals has not been performed in many areas of the world. Due to lack of funding or interest, many global governments have failed to update their charted shore's positioning.

Aboard our boat, we now have a set of slick digital charts on CD's, that run in our computer to generate a screen upon which our GPS position is shown by a little boat icon. But wait! Our position, derived by GPS, has us on the chart up on the hill in the middle of the highway above Marina Coral! Meanwhile we are still afloat and looking up the hill at our supposed position 1/3 mile northeast of us!

No, your GPS is not at fault, the chart you are using, whether a paper chart or a digital computer chart, is not correct in it's positioning of the land mass by latitude and longitude. These charts are in dire need of update but the task has yet to be performed. You may have noticed that Marina Coral does not yet exist according to the latest published chart we are using.

Final word on any navigational decision, GPS and chart positioning should not be overly relied upon. Your decisions must be made by reliance on all available means of observance of the situation. This includes radar, depth soundings, compass bearings of known landmarks, knowledge of current drift and wind effects, dead-reckoning of speed and position, and most importantly visual observation. Adding the GPS numbers and resultant chart position, as a last means of verifying all of the above, will probably keep you out of trouble. After all, what are you going to do if your GPS fails? At _all_ times of the passage, you must have a moment-to-moment grip on where you are by the most basic means of navigation handed down to us by the ancient True Travelers.

Ensenada Map Sites

*See our Site Maps for placement of these numbered locations to visit in Ensenada.

1.   Port Captain: Blvd. Azuela #101. Office of Immigration is next door to the southwest.

2.   Red Cross Hospital: 2 miles east of Marina Coral on Highway 1. Ambulance emergency service, US $5 minimum donation for care, drugs free if available.
Free calls for emergencies: 066-local 911; 060-local police; 112-federal police; 068-fire department.

3.   Banamex Bank: Ave. Ryerson #279. 1 block west of Ave. Ruiz and Hussong's. Remote, quiet location, usually not busy.

4.   Bancomer Bank: corner of Ave. Juarez and Ave. Riveroll. Large, busy downtown location, popular with tourists due to central location.

5.   Hussong's Cantina: Ave. Ruiz #113. Opened in 1892 by a German immigrant named Johan Hussong, and still owned by his son Juan has changed little aside from the addition of electricity. The walls display an outstanding collection of photography of times gone by. Famous for a sometimes boisterous and rowdy atmosphere, pierced by mariachi and ranchero musicians. One of the first establishments to allow women into a decidedly male institution, the Mexican Cantina.

6.   Baja Naval Marina & Boatyard: Ave. de la Marina #10. A modern boat yard offering all aspects of yacht repair and construction with a large travel lift and a clean, concrete floored enclosure. There are 50 slips and live aboard is permitted. Restrooms, electricity, water, laundry, and phone service are available with 24-hour security. Tel. 011-52(646)174-0020 Fax. 011-52(646)174-0028 Contact Diego Fernández or Guillermo Sarabia. E-mail:marina@bajanaval.com. Web Site:www.bajanaval.com

7.   Fish Market: A short walk west of Baja Naval along the waterfront. Open stalled market where the catch of the day is for sale at economy prices. Example-fresh swordfish for US $5 a kilo (2.2 pounds). You may find shrimp, lobster, yellowfin, yellowtail, albacore, dorado, halibut, shark, rockfish, etc..

8.   Bus Depot: Ave. Riveroll between 10th and 11th. The Marco Polo touring buses are the Boeing 747's of Mexico. A mid-night stop at one of the large bus stations in a major city reminds us of a scaled down Chicago O'Hare airport, complete with taco and hot dog stands, bustling with the excitement of wide-eyed True Travelers looking for their coach along the long line of idling, arriving and departing super cruisers. A ticket from Ensenada to La Paz one-way is around US $80; a wild 22 hour ride complete with movies on suspended TV's, stops for livestock on the road along the dark unlit Baja desert highway, a sunrise cruise along the incredibly beautiful Santa Rosalia to Puerto Escondido area on the Sea of Cortez, and a scary bathroom with eminating fumage. *Travel tips - Take the 2 pm bus to La Paz to time sunset over the Pacific Ocean at San Quintin, and sunrise over the Sea of Cortez at Santa Rosalia. Bring your own toilet paper and avoid sitting in the rear near the water closet.

9.   Parque Revolution (Revolution Park): Ave. Obregon and 6th. Large, one block tree shaded park with benches, child's play area, and a bandstand. The most traditional plaza in Ensenada; lively on

weekends and evenings with a festive family atmosphere.

10.   Gordo's, Juanito's, and Sergio's Sportsfishing: A short walk west from Baja Naval along the waterfront. For years, perhaps the greatest source of tourism dollars for Ensenada, these three businesses manage their own docks and a fleet of colorful craft fitted to catch "the big one". All the popular local fish varieties can be landed, the months of June thru September being the best for fishing with whale watching from December to April.

11.   Telefonica MoviStar-Baja Cellular: Blvd. Lazaro Cardenas #678. Local cellular service available. One of a chain, we like this one as it is centrally located next to other businesses we frequent. Tel. 178-23-11

12.   Pizza Hut: Next door to the Baja Cellular listed above. Tel. 178-18-88

13.   McDonalds Restaurant: Corner of Ave. Macheros and Blvd. Lazaro Cardenas. Across the street from Pizza Hut.

14.   Mini-mart Liquor Store: Next to the Pizza Hut and across the street from McDonalds. One of the largest liquor stores in town advertising the best prices.

15.   Alfonso's Pizza: On Macheros next to the above liquor store. Great pizza, locally owned shop. Tel. 178-87-52 or 174-05-70.

16.   Gastelum 57 Restaurant: Ave. Las Dunas 118. Wonderful Mediterranean cuisine; most meals US $10 or less. The cook was once the personal chef on a privately owned Mediterranean based mega-yacht and also a chef at a famous Beverly Hills restaurant. The presentation is a delight! Don't miss the fresh baked bread or tortilla soup. Intimate, romantic ambiance. Tel. 177-14-80

17.   Gigante Market: Ave. Gastelum 1/2 block north of Ave. Lopez Mateos. Closest Gigante market to Marina Coral; smaller than most, and typically un-crowded. Like all Gigantes, they accept major credit cards.

18.   Tortilleria Renteria: 2nd Street #558. Around the corner north from the Gigante market listed above. First established in 1935, this large, newly constructed building is home to a shop popular for many years. Fresh hot-off-the-conveyor belt corn tortillas sold by the kilo or half kilo. Pick up some of their fresh homemade cheese to roll in your hot tortillas along with a cerveza down at the harbor.

19.   Dr. J Miguel Rico Dentist: 7th Street #251. Across the street north from Parque Revolucion. A mean toothache brought us here. An extraction and two bridges later, I am pleased to be able to recommend this nice gentleman to you. Prices 1/3 to 1/4 of stateside pricing; always busy with locals and gringos. The doctor speaks some English, very friendly atmosphere. Tel. 174-08-33

20.   Domino's Pizza: Corner of 9th street and Ave. Ruiz. Tel. 178-83-00

21.   Panaderia La Mexicana: Ave. Gastelum #173. Across the street from the Gigante market listed above. Small, clean, always something baking in the back of the shop. Don't miss the fresh, slightly crispy and delightfully chewy, coconut macaroons piled on the tray next to the cash register.

22.   Caliente Sportsbook: next-door west of Baja Naval. A sterile atmosphere attractive to only those laying a bet or collecting winnings. Small bar, pari-mutuel horse race boards on the wall and cigarette smoke.

23.   San Nicholas Hotel: Ave. Guadalupe and Ave. Lopez Mateos. The largest hotel in Ensenada, built in the early 70's and refurbished in the last decade. This Aztec motif structure encloses a pool, underground disco, restaurant and a Caliente Sportsbook. Bring your dobbers as a large convention room fills with Bingo players a few nights a week. Two large dirt lots adjoin the hotel for the accommodation of cars with trailers. This is handy for those with boats or car trailers during the annual off-road races. Nico Saad, who was liaison to Ronald Reagan for 8 years as the Mexican State & Federal Director of Tourism, and a former Mexican national championship water-skier, is the owner. A very friendly gentleman open to all for conversation. We consider his personal office at the hotel the best "office of tourism" in Ensenada. You are encouraged to stop by and say hi, as he speaks fluent English. Ensenada Tel. 176-19-01 San Diego Tel. (619) 298-4105

24.   Asadero Angus Beef & Grill: Corner of 9th street and Ave. Gastelum. Large, clean open air beef market and carne asada grill.

25.   Angencia Arjona Hardware/True Value Store: Blvd. Azueta #106. Across from the Port Captain's Office. Excellent general hardware and marine hardware stock. Tel. 178-31-01

26.   Gordo's Boatyard: On the waterfront next-door east of the fish market. For years, this yard was only for service of the Gordo's sports fishing fleet. Now it is an alternative to other yards for haul out and repairs. They can service 2 to 3 boats at a time up to 70 feet in length. Boats are hauled in steel cradles on rubber tires after being floated into place over the center of the cradle. The harbor side walk transverses a steel drawbridge that is raised to permit the cradle to be pulled up the causeway by cable. Two of our friend's Choey Lee sailboats were hauled here for 3 months each, having bottom blister repair and teak decks replaced with fiberglass. Complete LP paint jobs were applied. Both were very satisfied and the cost was far lower than other local estimates and less than 1/2 of Stateside prices. Thereafter, our boat (another Cheoy Lee) was hauled for 8 weeks for blister dry-out and repair. Due to our previous referrals, we were given an excellent deal, the job was done efficiently and the bottom was coated with paint more effective than that allowed in the U.S.. Since then, a business associate's older wooden 60-foot powerboat was hauled to the owner's complete satisfaction. Currently, a 56-foot wood 1972 Bertram International sport fisher is close to completion after 2 years, undergoing a total reconstruction of the superstructure due to termite infestation, with decks having been replaced, a tower installed and a complete LP paint job. Paint and mechanical work are performed in the water at adjacent docks. Contact Herman at Gordo's or see Bernardo at the yard for information. They both speak excellent English. You will pay two bills; one from Gordo's for the haul out and lay days, and another to Bernardo for the yard work. Very competent, friendly and reasonable.

27.   Abarratera de Baja CA: Juarez and Blancarte #467. A large, well stocked store that reminds us of a Smart and Final or the Price Club. Great for stocking the boat before a long voyage. Tel. 178-35-18 and 178-22-48

28.   Tacos La Chispa: Ave. Lopez Mateos and Soto Street #2062. Very popular with the locals is this

cute little clean shop, with a simple approach to service. Carne asada tacos, burritos, and quesadillas are posted on the wall menu. You order at the register, pay, and wait for the best beef feast we've found, sprinkled with homemade beans, enclosed in homemade tortillas. Condiments are on the high cafeteria style tiled bar surrounding the family of cooks, servers and the hot grill. Open 12:30 pm to 11 pm, closed Tuesday. When disembarking passengers from the car, watch out for the high curbing in front of the restaurant.

29.   Movie Theaters: across the street and 1 block east of Tacos La Chispa. First run major movies in original format with Spanish subtitles. Usually a month or so after initial release and for less than US $5.

30.   Auto Detalia: corner of 7th street and Ave. Moctezuma. 1/2 block west of Dr. Rico dentist's office. Car wash, wax, and detail. Perfect to have done while your teeth are being fixed. Complete wash, wax, and detail of our VW van was less than US $50!

31.   La Luna Meat Market: corner of 9th street and Ave. Moctezuma. A small general convenience market with a fresh meat counter at the back of the store.

32.   Cruiseport Villiage Ship Terminal: At the waterfront where the Arroyo de Ensenada meets the harbor. Lots-a gringo dollars disembarking and lots-a Mexican trinkets being exported daily.

33.   Cruiseport Marina: Next to the cruise ship terminal and behind the Corona Hotel. The newest Marina to date of publication in Ensenada. Here you will find 200 slips, a close proximity to town, and all of the conveniences offered by California marinas. Cruiseport's creation will be positive, as it will enable more yacht owners to realize the benefits of the 90 Day Yacht Club. Live aboard is permitted and there is 24 hour security. Contact Jerry Wiseman or Carmen Castro. Tel. 011-52(646)173-41-41 Web Sites: www.eportvillage.com and www.ecpvmarina.com

34.   Post Office: On Ave. Juarez between Ave. Floesta and Ave. Espinoza. Unless you plan to be in Ensenada for an extended period of time, don't mail items north. A telephone call may be more effective. Your mail will probably arrive in the States after you return.

35.   Our Lady of Guadalupe Church: corner of Ave. Floresta and Ave. Juarez. Largest cathedral in Ensenada. Center of activity during religious festivities, and the site of many celebrations and processions.

36.   Corona Hotel: Corner of Blvd. Lazaro Mateos and Ave. Club Rotario. Expensive hotel situated on the harbor at the site of the new Cruiseport Marina. Excellent view rooms, overlooking the entire Ensenada harbor area.

37.   La Palapaloca Bar and Restaurant: Across the street from the Corona Hotel. Casual, open-air atmosphere with adjacent outdoor sand volleyball court overlooked by an outdoor deck. Most major boxing matches are shown on the many TV's at a price which includes tickets to buy food and drink.

38.   Hospital: One block down the hill to the west from the huge Gigante sign at the corner of Ave. Reforma and Calle Augustin Sangines. This hospital is listed if you need quick emergency care on the southeast end of town. The Red Cross Hospital (site #2) serves the northwest end of town.

39.   Gigante Market: Corner of Ave. Reforma and Calle Augustin Sangines, marked by a gigantic (Gigante) sign on the corner. We like this store because it is huge and festive, and the trip to and from includes a scenic drive along the harbor. Usually filled with loud Latino music with trays of free food throughout the store for your tasting pleasure. You'll find a bakery goods area, store made fresh whole rotisserie chickens, tortillas and salsa. A butcher style meat counter, a complete selection of liquors, hardware and home supplies, and a little cafeteria will be found at this full service Gigante location. The corner mall includes a video store, pizza shop and a selection of varied small local businesses. We usually travel to this market at around 10 am, as this is the time each day that liquor sales can begin, before the crowd arrives at this popular store.

40.   Las Conzuelas Restaurant and Bar: One block east of Blvd. Lazaro Mateos on Calle Augustin Sangines on the right side of the street. A favorite of many visiting Americans and local Ensenadans, a tasty selection of fine Mexican dishes will be found in a quiet, friendly, family atmosphere. Many nights include live entertainment.

41.   Naval Base: Corner of Ave. Reforma and Calle Augustin Sangines. Only listed here as a convenient landmark, admittance is barred to the general public.

42.   Marina Coral and Hotel: Km 103 on Highway 1D, #3421 Zona Playitas. This marina has 370 slips, all equipped for live aboard, and all the conveniences found at California marinas. The only fuel dock in Ensenada will be found here. See the section in our book that more completely describes this first class establishment. Yacht chandlery and mechanical repair shop on site. Referral to other yacht service businesses available at the Marina office. Dockmaster: Fito Espinoza. Office manager: Cynthia Romero. E-mail: marina@hotelcoral.com. Web Site: http:www.hotelcoral.com. You can contact the marina office on VHF Channel 71. Tel. 011-52(61)75-0000 Fax. 011-52(61)75-0005

43.   Quintas Papagayo Hotel and El Pelicano Restaurant: On Highway 1D just southeast of Coral Marina. A beachfront development owned and operated by the Hussong family. The grounds have a strange assortment of differing architecture and floor plans to choose from; most have kitchens, and some have fireplaces. You will enjoy experiencing the beachside quiet and tranquility, a treat when coming from busy California. Rented by the day, week, or month. A unit was occupied by friends that were hauled in Ensenada, with a kitchen, and a 3rd story south facing wrap-around-decked view of the entire Bahia Todos Santos, for US $600 a month. A similar beachfront California rent would be 3 to 4 times that amount. This site has tennis courts and a pool.Tel. (646)174-45-75 or (646)174-49-80

44.   Super Rapido Market: Small market with a selection of household goods and beer, 1/2 mile southeast of Coral Marina on Highway 1D. Closest convenience store to Marina Coral, delivery is available to your dock. Look for the large Tecate sign which marks the site. Tel. 174-54-00

45.   Pemex Gas Station: At the east end of the new bridge into Ensenada, on Blvd. Lazaro Cardenas. Large and friendly, full service.

46.   Juarez Monument: East end of Ave. Juarez at the Palacio Municipal. This statue marks the east end of town and the beginning of the trip to San Felipe. A common tribute found in many Mexican cities, to the beloved 19th century president of Mexico, Benito Juarez, born in Guelatao, Oaxaca. A national holiday in the spring, on March 21, celebrates his birthday.

47.   3 Heads Monuments: Plaza Civica or the Plaza de las Tres Cabezas, just north of Baja Naval on Blvd. Lazaro Cardenas at the foot of Ave. Riveroll. These three prominent gold statues of the heads of Benito Juarez, Miguel Hidalgo, and Venustiano Carranza, serve as a waypoint while describing the location of nearby locations. You may hear Ave. Riveroll called "the 3 heads street". Because the statues can be seen many blocks up the street into town, and is sometimes used as a reference to one's proximity in the downtown area. The plaza is the site of celebration on the weekends and holidays.

48.   Flagpole: In the plaza just east of Baja Naval on Ave. de la Marina. For the same reasons mentioned above, this also serves as a waypoint in describing the placement of nearby locations. Ave. Alvarado is known as "the flag street", as this landmark can be seen and utilized as a location reference almost anywhere in Ensenada, due to it's tremendous size. Standing 350 feet, it's interesting to note that this is the second largest flag in all of the Baja. The location of the largest bandera? You will see it flying proudly in Tijuana as you pass through en route to Ensenada.

49.   La Baguette: Blvd. Lazaro Cardenas #30 between Ave. Costillo and Ave. Blancarte. Simply the best french-style baguettes in Ensenada. You will often find them fresh and hot at 10 to 11 in the morning. Also, a selection of temptations fashioned to increase your daily calorie count, is on display and baked fresh daily.

50.   Tourist Information: 1/2 block east of the Corona Hotel on Blvd. Lazaro Cardenas. Maps, brochures and travel advice.

51.   Compu Club: Ave. Riveroll #143-7. This is perhaps the best computer Internet store in Ensenada, with other shops in Tijuana and Mexicali. They have computers available for you to e-mail friends and browse the Internet, within a very friendly, helpful atmosphere. In addition, they can set you up with an Internet connection on your boat.

52.   El Rey Sol Restaurant: Ave. Lopez Mateos #1000 at the Ave. Blancarte intersection. This family-owned establishment, founded in 1947, is a popular destination for those seeking a generous selection of French and Mexican cuisine. An outdoor, enclosed sidewalk area is the ideal location for afternoon crepes and espresso. Fresh baked on the premises, pastries are served in a patisserie area on lace-covered tables. Considered a bit pricey for some, the friendly and special atmosphere, and excellent food will serve to make up for the extra cost. Tel. 178-17-33

53.   Villalva Yacht Services: Ave. Alvarado #877. Home office location of Bernardo Villalva, who manages and owns the business described in the Gordo's boat yard section of this listing of Ensenada map sites. Bernardo will either be found here, Gordo's yard, or making a trip for supplies in San Diego. Printed estimates are available at no extra cost. Excellent work at a very reasonable cost by an honest gentleman that speaks fluent English. A sign on the upstairs rail marks the location. Beware of Oscar, the German shorthair watchdog, and try to hail someone from outside the tall iron fencing.

54.   Tornillos Alvarado: Calle Seta #1676. A small supply shop that has a complete selection of stainless steel nuts, washers and bolts, as well as general hardware. Some English spoken, with a good understanding of U.S. sizing of hardware, rather than metric sizing.

55.   Bronco's Steakhouse: Ave. Lopez Mateos #1525. Situated behind the San Nicholas Hotel. A Wild Western motif complete with hanging spurs and chaps, makes this off-the-beaten track restaurant seem a bit surreal. The mood is quiet and family oriented. Tel. 176-19-01

56.   Temo Tire Shop (Llantera Temo): Ave. Floresta and 2nd Street #190. We discovered this shop by accident. One of their servicemen was fixing someone else's flat tire at the Marina Coral, after we'd noticed a nail in one of our tires. The tire was still inflated, but too dangerous certainly for the trip back to San Diego. Our specially bought for Mexico, 8-ply tires helped save us on the trip down. 15 minutes later and the tire was repaired, for an asking charge of US $3! Needless to say we gave the serviceman 5 dollars, amazed at the low cost of the service. This repair is still going strong 30,000 miles later. Service at your location. Tel. 177-35-55

57.   Danny's Upholstrey: Ave. Floresta #245. Specializing in yachts, cars and motorhomes. Excellent low cost manufacture and repair of upholstrey items. See the owner, Felix Gutierrez. Tel. 176-59-78

58.   99-cent Store: Corner of Ave. Gastelum and 7th Street. Large store typical of this variety of store in the U.S..

59.   Dr. Miguel A. Ortiz Dentist: Ave. Gastelum #777-7. Endodontistry and Implantation Specialist exclusively. Instant computer imaging of your teeth and what problems you may have. Reconstruction of repaired areas available. Fluent English spoken by a friendly, personable doctor. Prices easily beat U.S. pricing. Tel. 178-37-77

60.   San Martin Pharmacy: Ave. Ruiz #780-790 at the corner of 8th Street. One of a chain throughout Ensenada. This is the largest store close to the Marina Coral. Open 24-hours with a 24-hour medical aid unit next door. Home delivery service available. Also has an office supply with copier and spiral binding service, a pay-per use phone on the premises, a lottery machine and a bottled water supply machine (bring your own 5 gallon container). Tel. 178-35-30 and 178-14-01

61.   Centro Social y Cultural: Large estate and building east of the Arroyo de Ensenada bridge on Ave. Lazaro Cardenas. Now a museum of Baja history, was once known as the Rivera del Pacifico Hotel, an infamous gambling establishment during the prohibition era in the U.S..

62.   Bodegas Santo Tomas: Ave. Miramar #666. This is the downtown winery and bottling plant for Santo Tomas Wines. A tour of the works and wine tasting of the product of Baja's oldest winery is available. The restaurant in the winery is known as one of Baja's finest. Cost US $1 for the tour. Tours Mon.-Sat. 11 am, 1 and 3 pm; Sun. 11 am and 1 pm. Tel. 178-33-33 -U.S. Tel. (619) 454-7166

63.   Napa Auto Parts: Corner of Ave. Blancarte and 9th Street. Easily recognized by the blue building and yellow logo common to U.S. Napa stores. Same generous stock of parts inside.

64.   Avalos Tire Shop (Llantera Avalos): Corner of Blancarte and 10th Street. Clean and modern tire shop. Service at your location. Tel. 178-23-93

65.   Industrial Electrical Supply (Equipos Electricos Industriales): Corner of Ave. Floresta and 9th Street. Large electrical supply store.

66.   Air Conditioning and Refrigeration Repair: Refrigeration Polo Norte at 11th Street between Ave. Miramar and Ave. Riveroll. Little blue building distinguished by a mural of houses, ships and cars, illustrating the scope of their service. Service at your location. Tel. 174-10-43

67.   Tourist information: Across the Blvd. Lazaro Cardenas from the Pemex listed above. Maps, brochures and travel advice.

68.   Angus Steak House: Just across the street northwest of the Naval Base at the corner of Blvd. Lazaro Cardenas and Calle Augustin Sangines. Great selection of prime cuts of butcher shop beef. The building, resembling our Black Angus Steak Houses in So. Cal., with a decidedly Mexican difference in menu.

69.   Hotel Playa: Ave. Lopez Mateos #540. Bargain priced and showing it's advanced age, but still offering a strategic location within the downtown shopping and partying area, this hotel offers nothing more than a room and a bed. Tel. 178-27-15

70.   Hotel Bahia: Blvd. Lazaro Cardenas and Ave. Alvarado. For many years a landmark on the downtown strip, this moderately priced hotel would tell quite a tale if enabled. Best rooms are the garden units located on the first floor. Cafe located on the premises. Tel. 178-21-03

71.   Restaurant Pekin: Ave. Ruiz #20. Specializing in Cantonese cuisine and takeout service. A mere US $4 will buy you a combination plate of food that you and a friend may have trouble finishing. Tel. 174-08-15 and 178-11-58

72.   ixtle Embroidery and Silkscreen: Virgilio Uribe #465. If you want to supply your family and crew with some smartly embroidered or silkscreened shirts, hats or other assorted boat gear; this is the place to visit. Bring your own apparel and logo design, or they can supply the materials from their catalogue. An appendage of a very fine silver, guitar and leather corporation, Mario's, established in 1970. Shops in Ensenada and Cancun. Contact Mauricio Cantu at mcantu@telnor.net. Tel. 178-83-88

Points of Interest Driving South

The following is a list of places we have stopped and evaluated on our many trips to and from Ensenada. Most are presented with the kilometer number as designated by the nearest marker by the side of the road. On both the free and toll roads, you will find these kilometer markers. Note that the toll road numbers read 7 kilometers more due to the greater distance traveled on that road from the border.

In Mexico, we start at the south end of Rosarito Beach. While traveling through Rosarito you will find a busy roadside arcade of pottery, tile, ceramic, iron sculpture, and upholstery shops. We usually travel through Tijuana and Rosarito as quickly as possible. We find the mood much more relaxed and the prices increasingly better as we exit the border belt.

First, we will give you a few tips about stops you may need to make in the U.S. before you cross into Mexico.

Palm Avenue, the Highway 75 exit to Imperial Beach from I-5: This is the last easy-return exit before the border that supplies the most diverse range of businesses.

Immediately after you exit to the west, there is a shopping center with a Bank of America, a Home Depot, and a large grocery store on your right. After the first light traveling west, a gas station with very competitive gas pricing is available for a top off of fuel for your tank before crossing the border. Two long blocks up Palm to the west on the left, you will find a 7-11 with gas pumps that accept credit cards and are usually within a few pennies of the other station's pricing.

On Palm, you will find most any type of fast food you may be craving before crossing into Mexico or upon your return. Do not fail to stop at the Farm Fresh Market across the street from the gas station just before the intersection that leads you onto the freeway south. This is a genuinely classic locally owned store with an all purpose supply of products, complete with a great selection of freshly butchered beef and pork, bulk cheeses, vegetables, and a hot food counter. We usually load up on beef for bar-be-ques, some of their hot beans and rice and fresh made chips to cover our first meals at the boat before shopping in Mexico. If you are only going south for the few days, you will find everything you need here. Some wine and beer bought in Ensenada should complete your meals for your visit to the 90 Day Yacht Club.

San Ysidro Blvd.: The last stop for car insurance covering your car in Mexico will be found here. It is expensive to insure for only a few days and the cost is based on the value of your car. If you plan to spend quite a bit of time in Mexico, it is best to find a six month or annual policy from a reputable California insurance broker. Avoid crossing under the freeway to San Ysidro, as this is a very busy border town that you will be glad you missed.

We now will progress to points in Mexico...

As you approach any of the three toll plazas, you will see a sign that reads "caseta de cobro", warning you to expect a toll stop. Remember, the toll must be paid in total in only one currency. In addition, on the road signs along the way, cuota means toll and libre means free as designations for the two parallel roads. Before you enter and have to pay at the Rosarito plaza, a large green exit sign on the toll road listing Las Rocas as the bottom line of other listed destinations bears you off to the right and onto the free road. If you happen to miss this exit, you can cut through the Pemax station at the Rosarito toll plaza to join the free road. This enables you to bypass paying that toll and travel through the roadside businesses listed and following in our text. Our explanation from here will take the free road route in describing the stops along the way, but all these stops beyond Puerto Nuevo are accessible from the toll road and we will give you exit names when necessary to access these locations. However, if you continue on the toll road through the Rosarito toll plaza, you will miss all the locations mentioned below until you reach Puerto Nuevo, as there are no exits before that point. The kilometer numbers given are the distances on the markers on the free road until the La Mision exit where we will continue with the toll road kilometer marker numbers.

Soon after passing around the Rosarito toll plaza on the free road, you will leave behind the last roadside stops that are an extension of Rosarito. At KM-33, you will see a large gated enclosure, which surrounds the Fox Studios where the movie Titanic was filmed. It is interesting to note that if you look closely while watching the film, over the silhouettes of characters supposedly at sea on a luxury liner, you will see the kelp beds that line the shores of Popotla, the little town next-door that hosted the event. The ship was built on the cliffs neighboring Popotla, and an instant boomtown was created for the duration of the filming of the movie.

Just south of the studio enclosure there is a large concrete arch. Passing under this arch on the dirt road will take you to the waterfront where you will find 30 or so colorful seafood stands. The catch of the day is the specialty of these homegrown and owned shops that remind us of Puerto Nuevo 35 years ago. Fresh out of the local fishing boats you will have your choice of lobster, crab, barracuda, sea urchins, clams, oysters, or octopus cocktails stored in coolers and prepared as you wait. Prices on the prepared food are less than Puerto Nuevo and Ensenada restaurants, but unprepared seafood is found less expensive at the Ensenada fish market. You are in the no frills zone here; the lack of electricity in most of these establishments causes them to close by sundown.

Next you will see the multi-story building un-occupied on Punta Descanso. You may have noticed, upon close inspection, that this expensive vacant structure appears to be leaning curiously to the south. Here we have our own local leaning tower of Descanso! This is a great landmark when navigating offshore, which is shown on our Navigation South Map.

Just around the point to the left is Calafia at KM-35, a self-proclaimed historical site. A hotel with 72 rooms perched on the cliffs, a restaurant, plus shops offering various goods will be found here. This is truly the best view of the next segment of the trip, and a stop here is recommended. We used to come here in the 60's, for the sole purpose of having a wonderful lobster lunch, accompanied by a magnificent view of the coast to the south.

KM-36 and KM-38: These are two surf spots we used to enjoy before the population explosion led us into the era we have now, of overcrowding and rude behavior by Gringo and Mexican surf Nazis. The waves seem to have been much better then, as the bottom contours changed with the adjacent land developments, amending the behavior and shape of the waves. Where now there are gated hotels, we once camped out in the open on undeveloped bluffs, washed by perfect point breaks, and enclosed by kelp beds which kept the waves glassy all day long. If you pick the right swell and are here midweek, fun waves can still be had.

Km-41 (Km 48 on the toll road): El Zarape grocery store, pharmacy, and bar and grill; This newly constructed two-story building is hard to miss in the Las Gaviotas area. We have found it to be much too pricey; they must have paid a lot for all that bright new paint. However, it is by far the most modern establishment of its kind between Rosarito and Ensenada. A collection of nice pottery goods can also be found here. We use this location as a landmark to tell us one of our most favorite stops is coming up around the next corner.

KM-41&1/2 (Km 48&1/2 on the toll road): Tamales Las Gaviotas; A sign advertising rooms for rent and tamales on a simple 2 story white and light green building marks our favotite food stop along the entire route to Ensenada. For 12 years this family-owned establishment has offered rooms and tamales to those passing by on the old road to Ensenada. Maria Cristina and Francisco welcome you from the window of their kitchen from which they serve the best chicken, cheese, and fruit HOT tamales we have ever tasted! Whether taken to go to your boat, or eaten at the yard furniture tables by the kitchen window, we advise you have refreshment close by to accent the savoring of these works of culinary art. We usually get a few extra to feed to the microwave en route to our mouths at the boat.

Km-43 (Km 50 on the toll road): Raul's Bar and Restaurant; Rooms for rent, with outdoor dining available at the restaurant. This is the first onramp to the toll road after bypassing the toll plaza at Rosarito. You can continue on south from here by either road, with many off ramps from the toll road to the next spots mentioned along the way. When traveling north (just after passing Puerto Nuevo), this will be the off ramp from the toll road to by-pass the Rosarito toll plaza or to stop at any of the above locations, and you can get back on the toll road after the tollbooths at Rosarito. This makes traveling the toll road free after the San Miguel plaza to the toll plaza closest to the border and the termination of the toll road going north. Alternatively, if you take the La Gloria turnoff and the free road over the hill to Tijuana, you can travel without a toll all the way to the border from San Miguel!

Km-44 (Km 51 on the toll road): Puerto Nuevo and the Newport Hotel; This is the place if you desire some action with a few hundred other tourists surrounding you seeking the same. Some relief from the crowds can be had during the week. The lobster dinners have gotten more expensive but the ambiance and experience are still the same in this now self-contained road stop.

Km-49 (Km 56 on the toll road): Vivero La Central; An expansive nursery with a huge selection of tropical plants and flowers located between the toll and free road. The toll road exits are the Puerto Nuevo/Cantamar off ramp when traveling from the north and the Cuenca Lechera exit from the south.

Km-52 (Km 59 on the toll road): Halfway House; Established in 1922 when the area south of Tijuana to Cabo San Lucas was connected by only dirt roads. This restaurant marked the halfway point to Ensenada from Tijuana and was a welcome stop during the long trip on the barely passable ruts called roads. Exit the Cuenca Lechera exit from the north and the La Mision exit from the south.

Km-59 (Km 66 on the toll road): La Mision and LaFonda; Restaurants, bars, hotels, liquor store, old mission site, camping and surfing at the La Mision exit. Here you can exit to the old free road south and bypass the San Miguel plaza, after a pleasant two-lane trip through the mountains east of the toll road south of Punta Salsipuedes. We will continue our commentary now while traveling on the toll road with the indicated kilometers numbers that are on the toll road markers.

Km-69: Area de Descanso; Roadside rest at a large beach with ample parking, bathrooms, horseback riding, and roadside snacks. The free road runs inland from this point south so no more toll road exits are necessary to mention. All the following sites are serviced by their own exits.

Km-73: Baja Seasons Trailer Park and Hotel; Large modern park with hookups, concrete parking and located right on the beach in a beautiful isolated area. Also offering beachfront cottages.

Km-73&1/2: Puerto La Salina; New marina and housing development currently under construction.

Km-77: Bajamar Ocean Front Golf and Resort; 1st class development located on a bluff overlooking the sea. Close enough to commute from Ensenada for an early morning Tee time. Arrangements can be made at Marina Coral.

Km-84: El Mirador; Closed restaurant and roadside rest marked by bright pink, green and yellow buildings. A must stop for the view south which offers a vista that reaches all the way to Punta Colonet on a clear day. This is perhaps the best scenic view on the entire trans-peninsular highway. Bathrooms are available. This is a landmark on our Navigation South Map and is located on Punta Salsipuedes.

Km-87: Salsipuedes; Camping, hiking, surfing, kayaking, in an isolated area. Cabins on the cliffs above the beach rent for under US $50 a night. Camping for US $6 a night with running water and no electricity.

Km-94: Playa Saldamando; Camping, hiking, surfing, kayaking, in an isolated area. Camping for US $6 to $8 a night with running water and no electricity.

Km-94&1/2: Mirador de Ballenas; Whale watching spot during the migration season of December to April; bathrooms and roadside rest.

Km-99: San Miguel toll plaza.

Km-99: San Miguel; Our favorite surf spot in past decades, now a crowded place on any day the surf is more than 3 feet. Camping, restaurant, house and trailer rental, bathrooms, hot showers and surfing at a price of a few dollars a day. Overnight camping on the beach US $8, trailer sites with hookup-US $12. Trailers sometimes available for US $30 a night.

Km-102 to 104: the town of El Sauzal.

Km-104: Hotel California; Quaint beachside hotel and surf spot. Overnight stay with hookup is US $10.

Km-104: Romona Beach Trailer Park and Motel; Beachside trailer park, motel and little store. Overnight stay with hookup is US $9.

Km-106: Las Rosas Hotel and Restaurant; Beautiful location on the cliffs overlooking the ocean with a sweeping view of the Bahia Todos Santos.

Km-106: Propane supplier (gas in Spanish).

Km-107: King Coronita Trailer Park; Located on the bluff above a little rocky beach, overlooking Coral Marina to the east, this park is perhaps one of the best kept secrets in Ensenada. Many residents have lived here for years in beachside trailer homes that command an incredible view of Bahia Todos Santos. Some of our marina friends live in the park, paying rates that are far lower than one might expect, even by Mexican standards.

Km-107: Marina Coral; See previous chapter describing this location.

Km-109: Ensenada.

Map Library

Cruiseport Marina

not to be used for navigation

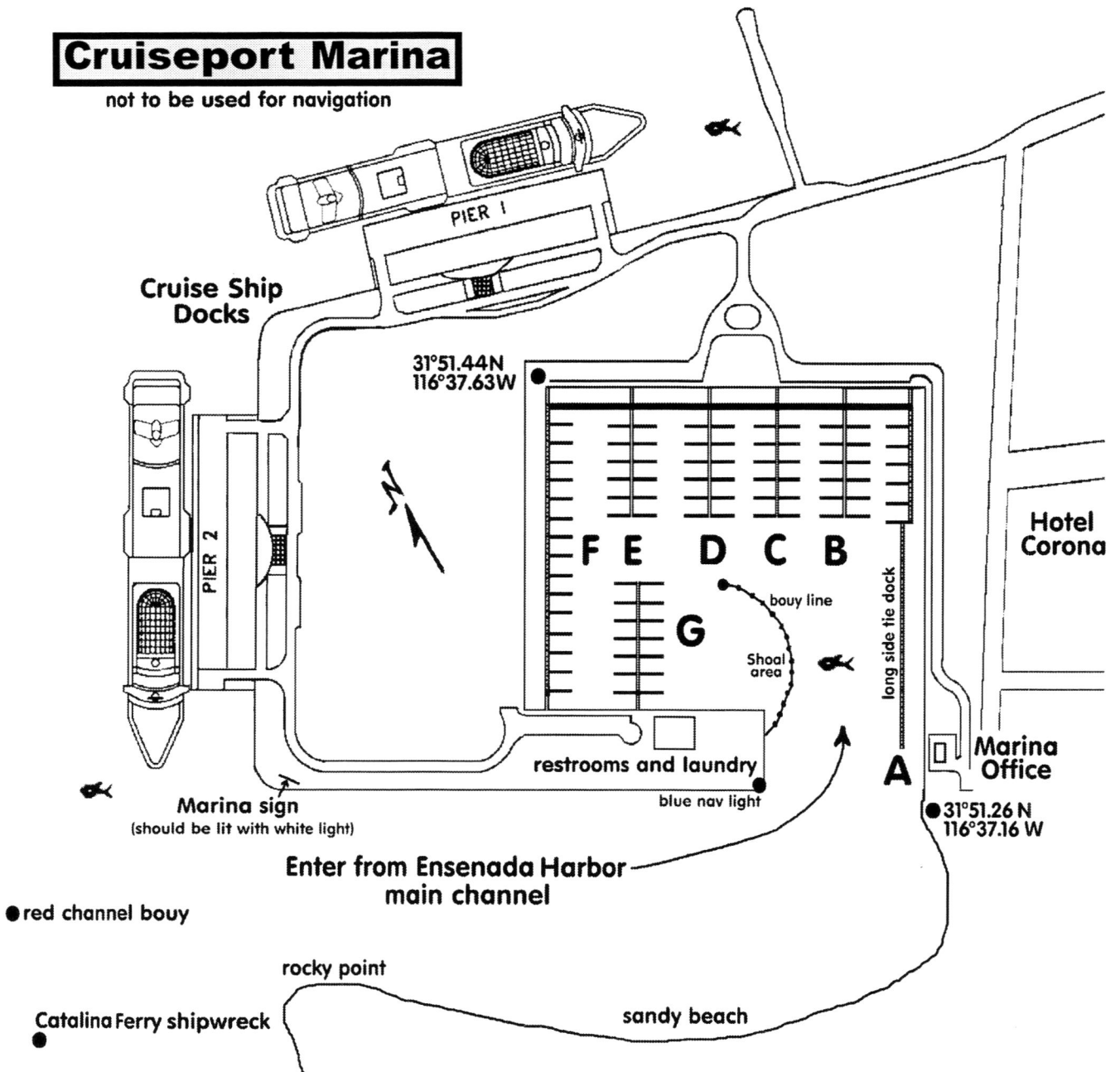

Cruise Ship
Docks

PIER 1

PIER 2

31°51.44N
116°37.63W

N

F E D C B

G

bouy line

Shoal
area

long side tie dock

restrooms and laundry

blue nav light

A

Hotel
Corona

Marina
Office

31°51.26 N
116°37.16 W

Marina sign
(should be lit with white light)

Enter from Ensenada Harbor
main channel

● red channel bouy

rocky point

Catalina Ferry shipwreck
●

sandy beach

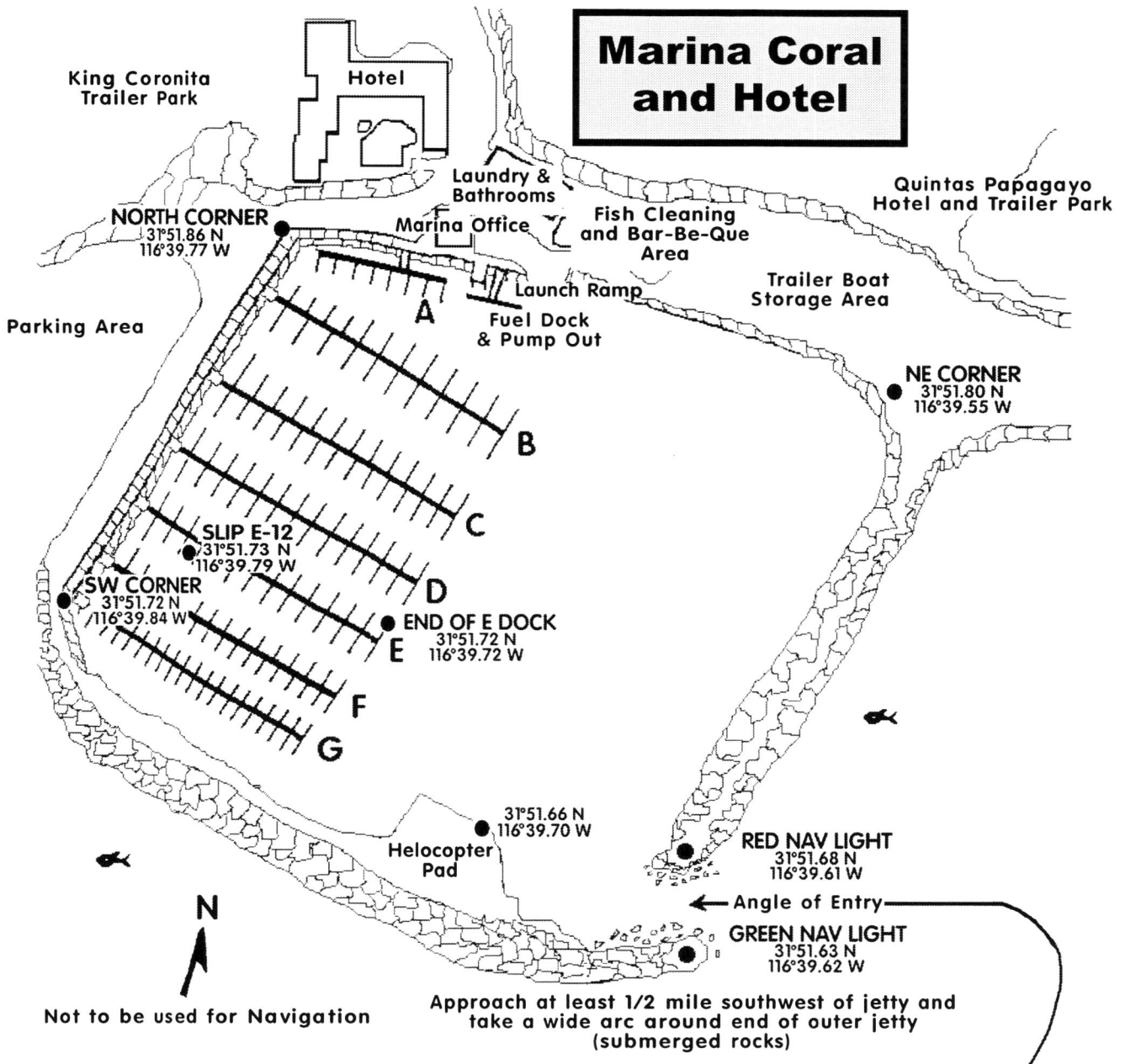

Marina Coral and Hotel

King Coronita Trailer Park

Hotel

Laundry & Bathrooms

Marina Office

Fish Cleaning and Bar-Be-Que Area

Quintas Papagayo Hotel and Trailer Park

NORTH CORNER
31°51.86 N
116°39.77 W

Parking Area

Launch Ramp

Fuel Dock & Pump Out

Trailer Boat Storage Area

NE CORNER
31°51.80 N
116°39.55 W

A

B

C

SLIP E-12
31°51.73 N
116°39.79 W

D

SW CORNER
31°51.72 N
116°39.84 W

END OF E DOCK
31°51.72 N
116°39.72 W

E

F

G

31°51.66 N
116°39.70 W

Helocopter Pad

RED NAV LIGHT
31°51.68 N
116°39.61 W

Angle of Entry

GREEN NAV LIGHT
31°51.63 N
116°39.62 W

N

Not to be used for Navigation

Approach at least 1/2 mile southwest of jetty and take a wide arc around end of outer jetty (submerged rocks)

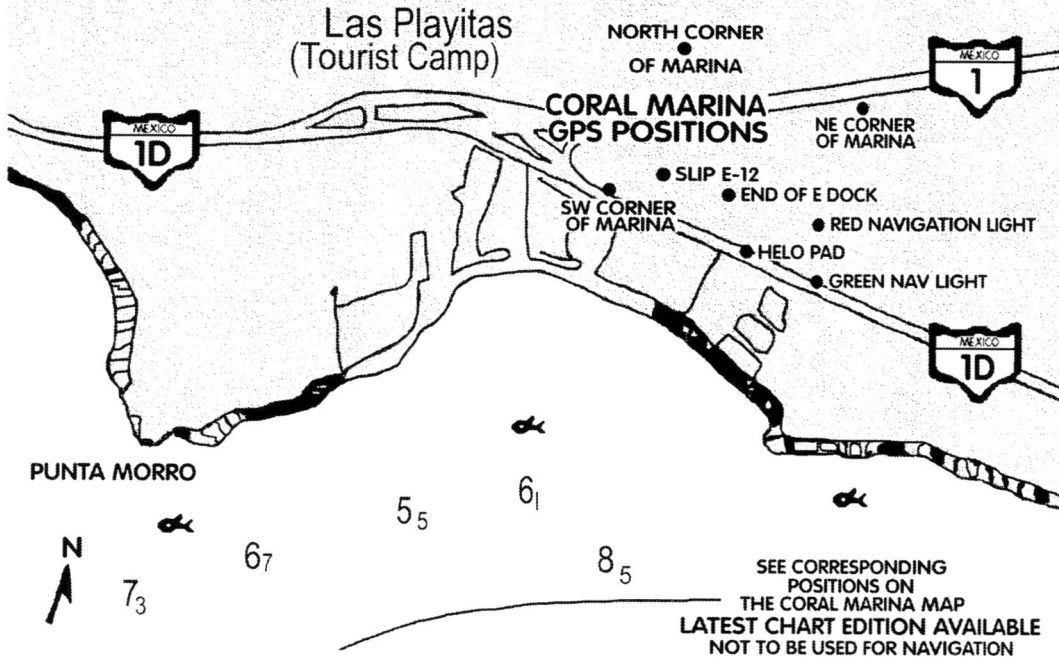

Chart #21021 GPS Position Inaccuracy

Las Playitas
(Tourist Camp)

NORTH CORNER
OF MARINA

**CORAL MARINA
GPS POSITIONS**

NE CORNER
OF MARINA

SLIP E-12

END OF E DOCK

SW CORNER
OF MARINA

RED NAVIGATION LIGHT

HELO PAD

GREEN NAV LIGHT

PUNTA MORRO

6_1

5_5

8_5

6_7

7_3

N

SEE CORRESPONDING
POSITIONS ON
THE CORAL MARINA MAP
LATEST CHART EDITION AVAILABLE
NOT TO BE USED FOR NAVIGATION

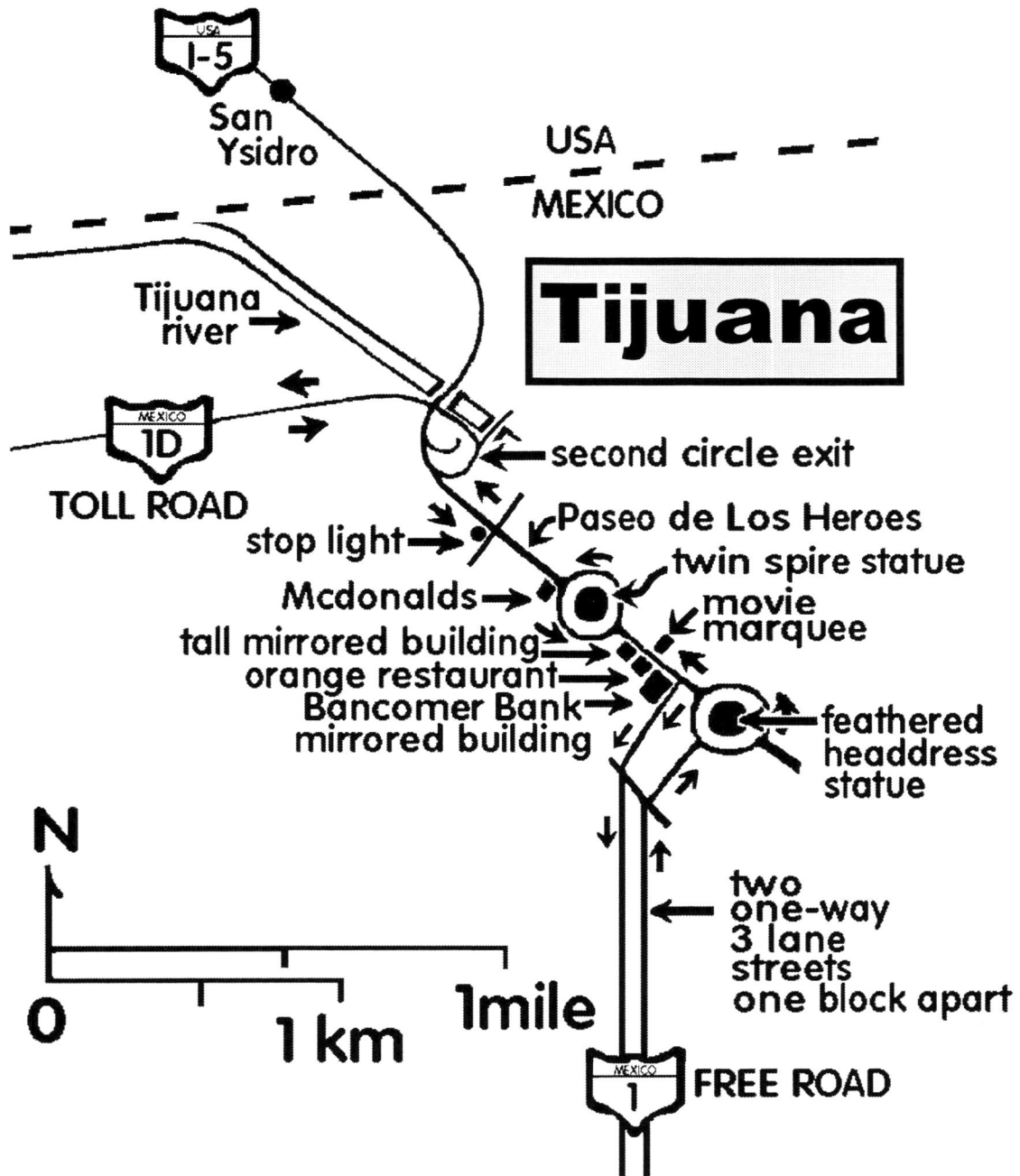

USA
I-5

San Ysidro

USA
- - -
MEXICO

Tijuana river →

MEXICO
1D

TOLL ROAD

Tijuana

second circle exit ←

stop light →

Paseo de Los Heroes

twin spire statue

Mcdonalds →

movie marquee

tall mirrored building →

orange restaurant →

Bancomer Bank →

mirrored building

feathered headdress statue

N

0   1 km   1mile

two one-way 3 lane streets one block apart

MEXICO
1   FREE ROAD

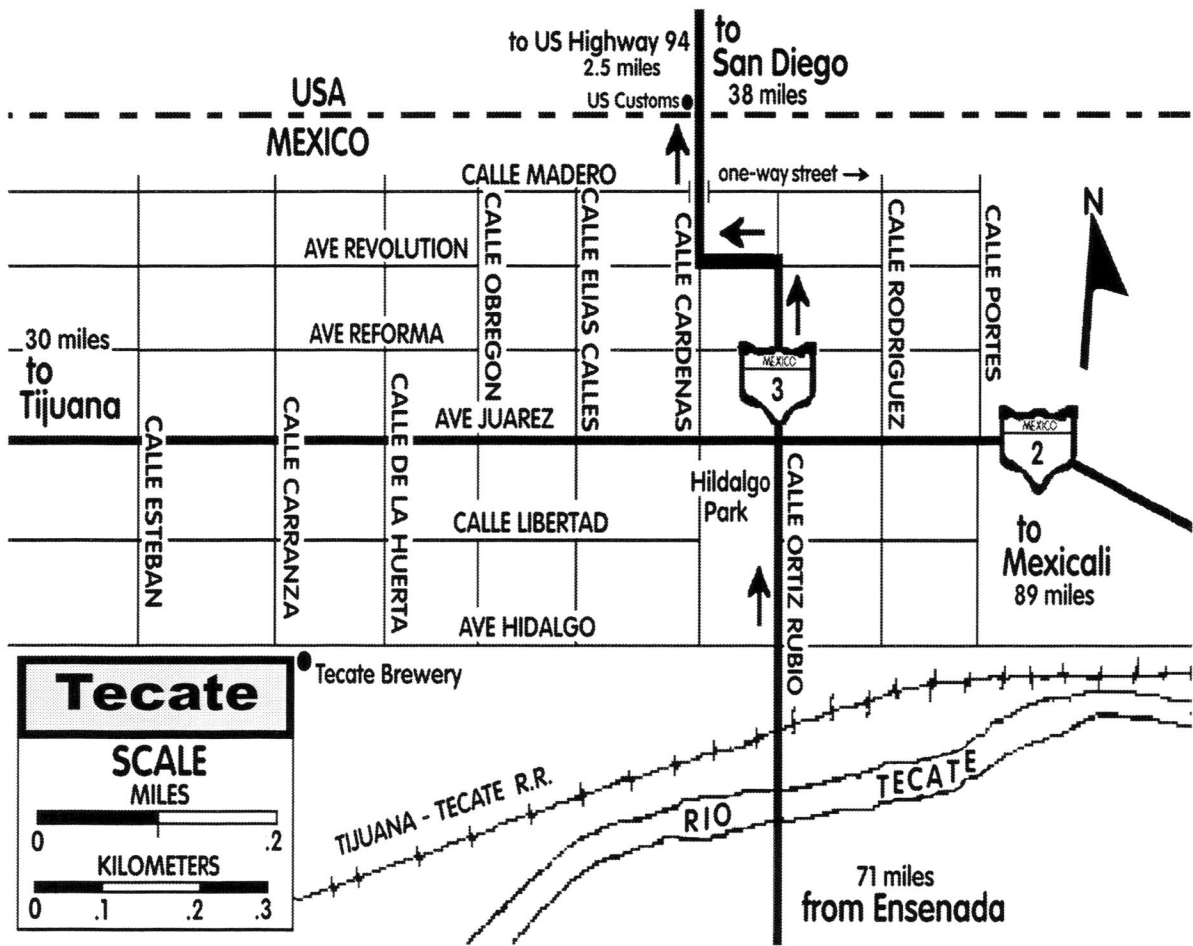

to US Highway 94
2.5 miles
to San Diego
38 miles
US Customs ●

USA
MEXICO

CALLE MADERO
one-way street →

AVE REVOLUTION

AVE REFORMA

30 miles
to
Tijuana

AVE JUAREZ

MEXICO 3

MEXICO 2

to
Mexicali
89 miles

CALLE OBREGON
CALLE ELIAS CALLES
CALLE CARDENAS
CALLE RODRIGUEZ
CALLE PORTES

CALLE ESTEBAN
CALLE CARRANZA
CALLE DE LA HUERTA
CALLE ORTIZ RUBIO

CALLE LIBERTAD

Hildalgo
Park

AVE HIDALGO

N

Tecate
● Tecate Brewery

SCALE
MILES
0   .2
KILOMETERS
0   .1   .2   .3

TIJUANA - TECATE R.R.

RIO
TECATE

71 miles
from Ensenada

Bullring by the Sea

Tijuana

USA

Islas Coronados

San Antonio

La Gloria

MEXICO

US Highway 94

Rosarito

Tecate

Popotla

Punta Descanso

Calafia

106km

Puerto Nuevo

Valle de las Palmas

Halfway House

Km 48
El Testerazo

La Mision

MEXICO
3

La Salina

109 km

Bajamar

MEXICO
1D

Domeco Winery

Km 63
EJ. Ignacio Zaragoza

MEXICO
1

Punta Salsipuedes

Km 73
Guadalupe
only Pemex
on this road
until Tecate

L A Cetto Winery

Punta San Miguel

Islas
Todos Santos

3km

El Sauzal

Ensenada

Bahia de
Todos Santos

Punta Banda

MEXICO
3

La Bufadora

to San Felipe

Maneadero

Agua
Caliente

to San Quintin

Not to be Used for Navigation

SYMBOLS

Surfing	
International Airport	
Local Airport	
Diving	
Beach	
Free Road	
Mileage Marker	
Toll Road	
Mission	
Scenic View	
Toll Booth	

Regional Roadmap

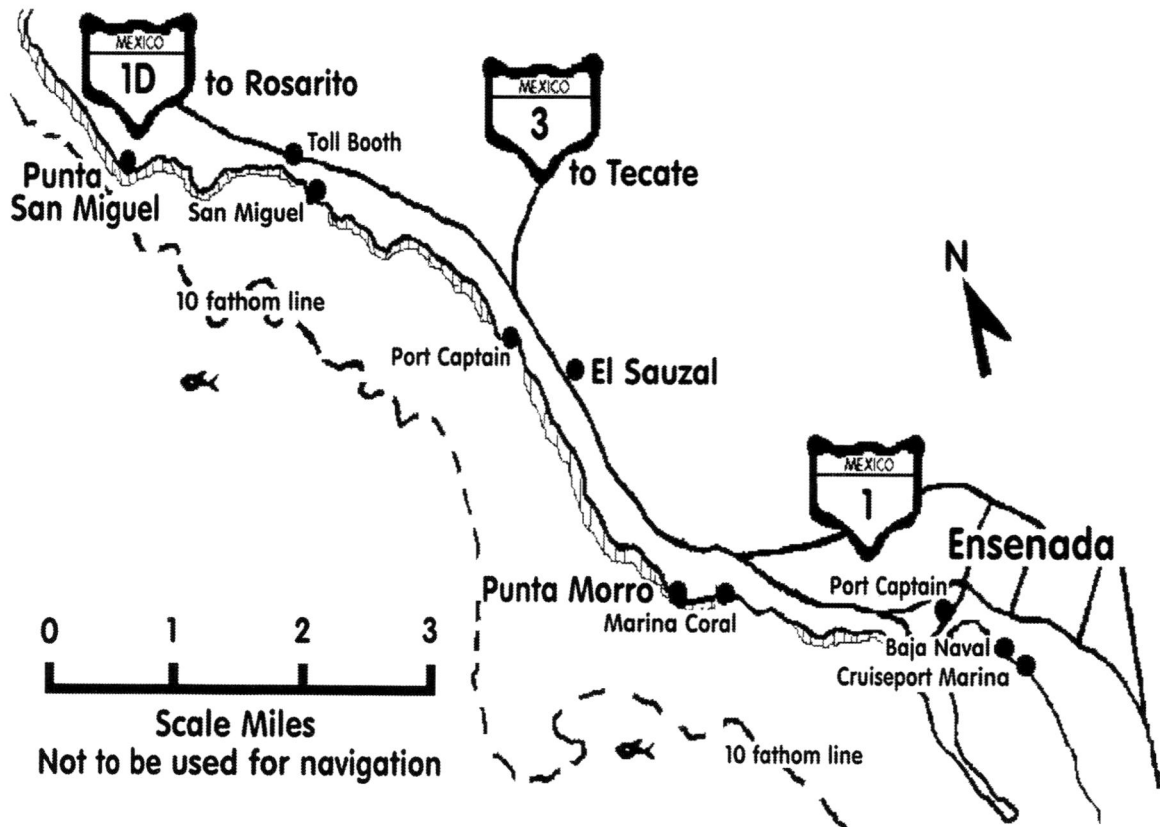

MEXICO 1D to Rosarito

Toll Booth

Punta San Miguel

San Miguel

10 fathom line

MEXICO 3 to Tecate

Port Captain

El Sauzal

N

MEXICO 1

Ensenada

Punta Morro

Port Captain

Marina Coral

Baja Naval

Cruiseport Marina

10 fathom line

0 1 2 3

Scale Miles
Not to be used for navigation

**Ensenada to San Miguel
Roadmap**

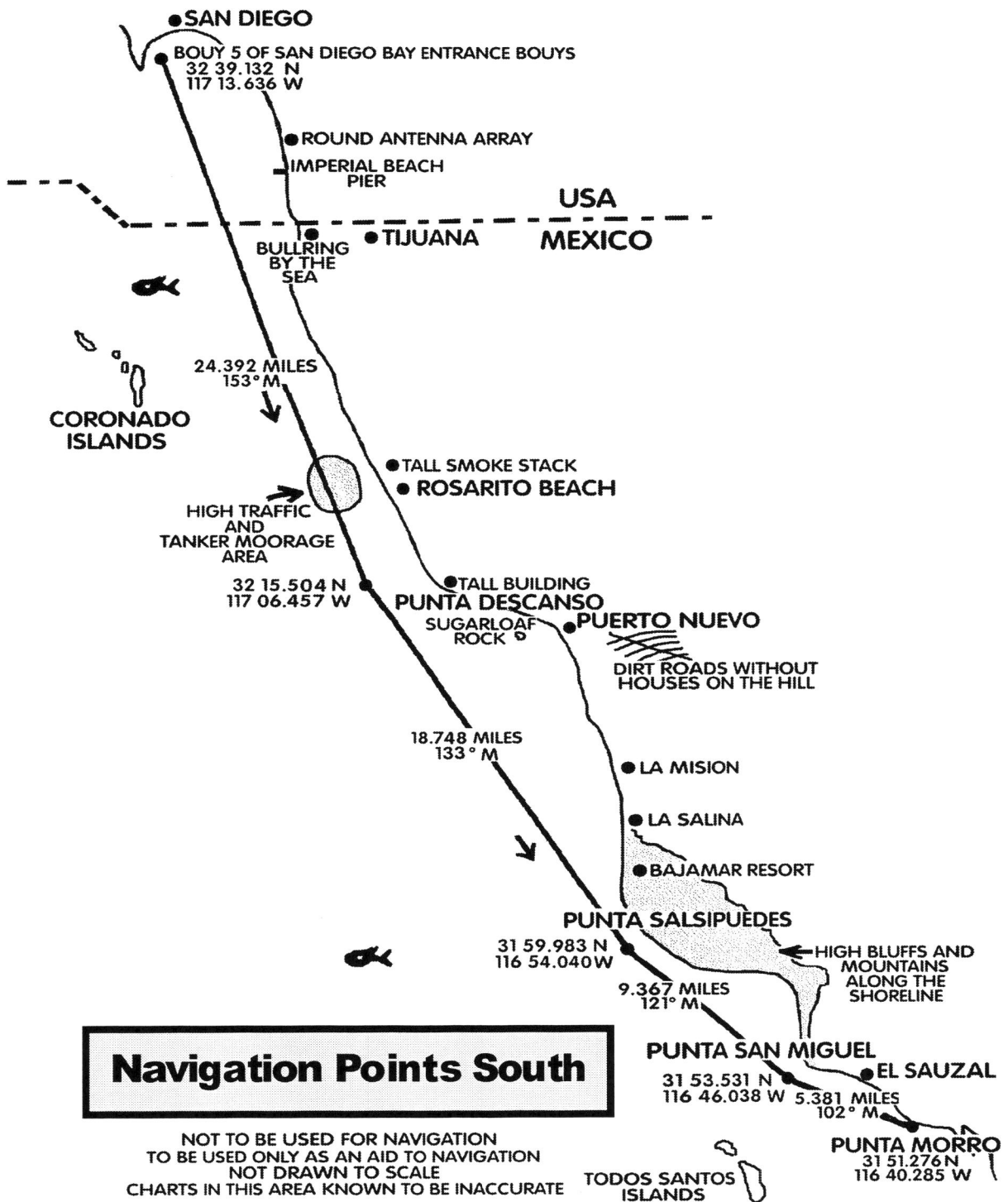

SAN DIEGO

BOUY 5 OF SAN DIEGO BAY ENTRANCE BOUYS
32 39.132 N
117 13.636 W

ROUND ANTENNA ARRAY

IMPERIAL BEACH
PIER

USA

BULLRING BY THE SEA

TIJUANA

MEXICO

24.392 MILES
153° M

CORONADO ISLANDS

TALL SMOKE STACK

ROSARITO BEACH

HIGH TRAFFIC AND TANKER MOORAGE AREA

32 15.504 N
117 06.457 W

TALL BUILDING

PUNTA DESCANSO

SUGARLOAF ROCK

PUERTO NUEVO

DIRT ROADS WITHOUT HOUSES ON THE HILL

18.748 MILES
133° M

LA MISION

LA SALINA

BAJAMAR RESORT

PUNTA SALSIPUEDES

31 59.983 N
116 54.040 W

HIGH BLUFFS AND MOUNTAINS ALONG THE SHORELINE

9.367 MILES
121° M

PUNTA SAN MIGUEL

EL SAUZAL

31 53.531 N
116 46.038 W

5.381 MILES
102° M

Navigation Points South

PUNTA MORRO
31 51.276 N
116 40.285 W

NOT TO BE USED FOR NAVIGATION
TO BE USED ONLY AS AN AID TO NAVIGATION
NOT DRAWN TO SCALE
CHARTS IN THIS AREA KNOWN TO BE INACCURATE

TODOS SANTOS ISLANDS

PUNTA SALSIPUEDES

● PINK AND YELLOW
BUILDINDS ON THE BLUFF

31 59.983 N
116 54.040 W

SEASIDE MOUNTAINS

TOLL ROAD

9.367 MILES
121° M

PUNTA SAN MIGUEL

COMMERCIAL FISHING PORT
AND FISH PROCESSING PLANT

31 53.531 N
116 46.038 W

● EL SAUZAL

5.381 MILES
102° M

LARGE WHITE TANKS
ON THE HILL

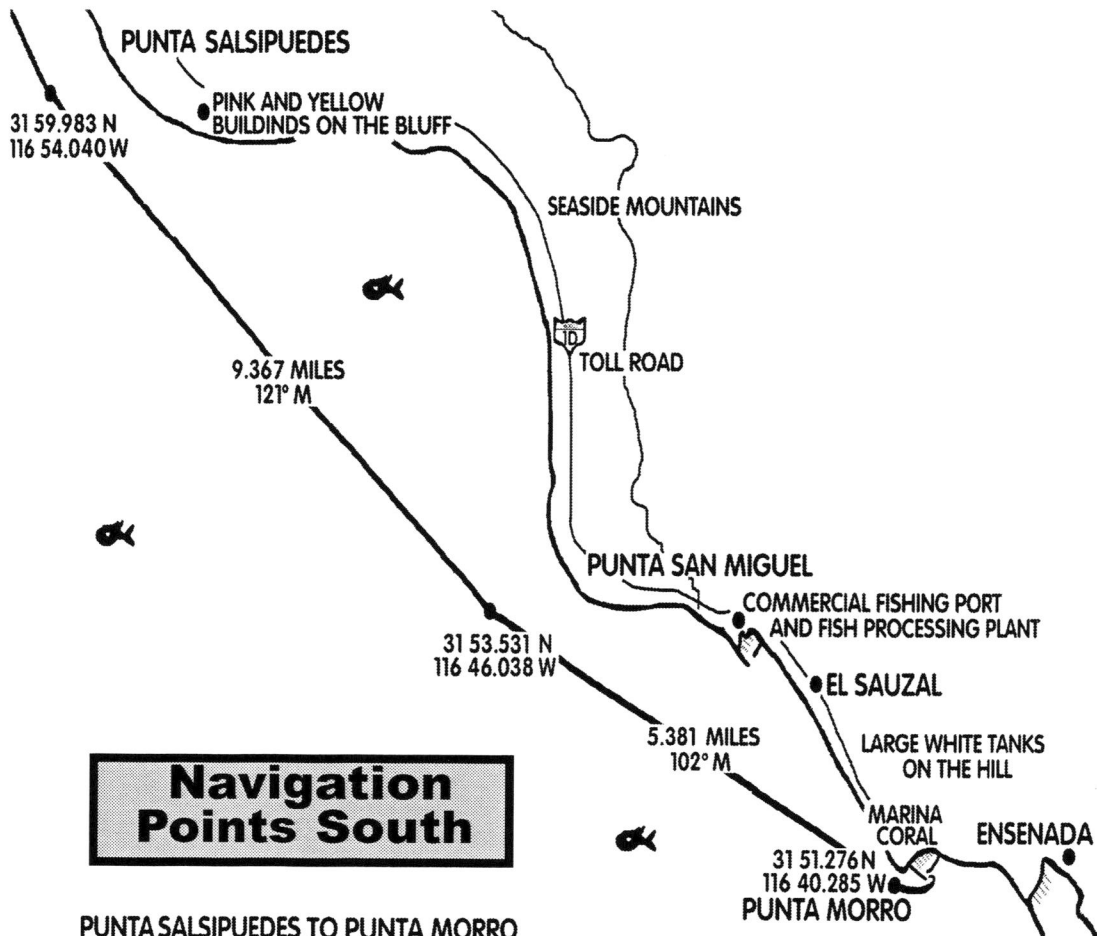

**Navigation
Points South**

MARINA
CORAL

ENSENADA

31 51.276 N
116 40.285 W

PUNTA MORRO

PUNTA SALSIPUEDES TO PUNTA MORRO

NOT TO BE USED FOR NAVIGATION
TO BE USED ONLY AS AN AID TO NAVIGATION
NOT DRAWN TO SCALE
CHARTS IN THIS AREA KNOWN TO BE INACCURATE

Ensenada Site Map

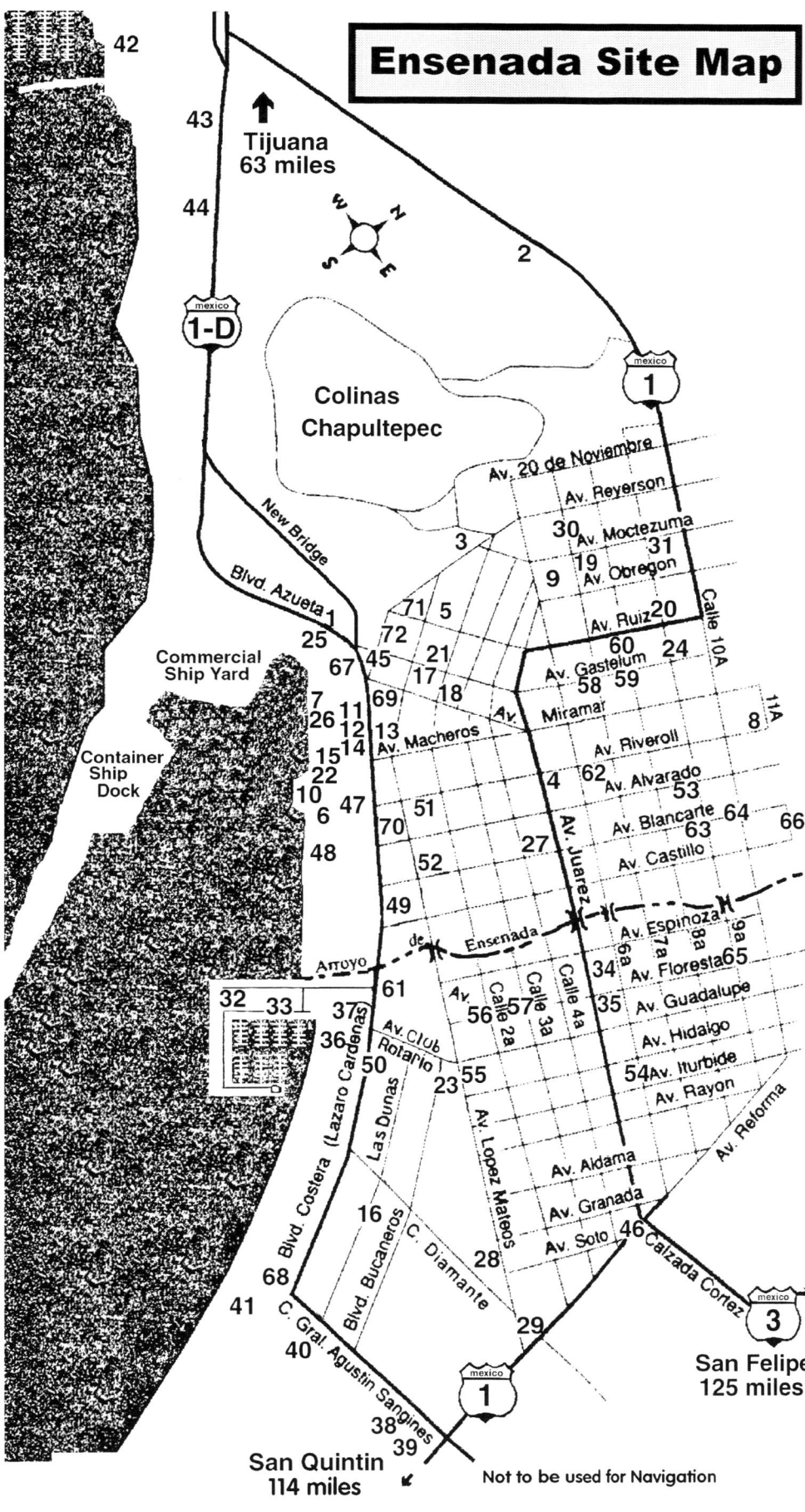

Tijuana
63 miles

1-D mexico

New Bridge

Blvd. Azueta

Colinas
Chapultepec

Av. 20 de Noviembre

Av. Reyerson

Av. Moctezuma

Av. Obregon

Av. Ruiz

Av. Gastelum

Av. Miramar

Av. Macheros

Av. Riveroll

Av. Alvarado

Av. Blancarte

Av. Castillo

Av. Juarez

Calle 10A

Commercial
Ship Yard

Container
Ship
Dock

Ensenada

de

Arroyo

Av. Espinoza

Av. Floresta

Av. Guadalupe

Av. Hidalgo

Av. Iturbide

Av. Rayon

Av. Reforma

Av. Club
Rotario

Av. Lopez Mateos

Calle 2a
Calle 3a
Calle 4a

Blvd. Costera (Lazaro Cardenas)

Las Dunas

Blvd. Bucaneros

C. Diamante

C. Gral. Agustin Sangines

Av. Aldama

Av. Granada

Av. Soto

Calzada Cortez

San Felipe
125 miles

mexico 3

San Quintin
114 miles

mexico 1

Not to be used for Navigation

1. Port Captain & Immigration
2. Red Cross Hospital
3. Banamex Bank
4. Bancomer Bank
5. Hussong's Cantina
6. Baja Naval
7. Fish Market
8. Bus Depot
9. Parque Revolution
10. Gordo's, Juanito's, &
    Sergio's Sportfishing
11. Baja Cellular
12. Pizza Hut
13. McDonalds
14. Mini Mart Liquor Store
15. Alfonso's Pizza
16. Gastelum 57 Restaurant
17. Gigante Market
18. Tortilleria Renteria
19. Doctor Rico Dentist
20. Domino's Pizza
21. Panaderia La Mexican
22. Caliente Sportsbook
23. San Nicholas Hotel
24. Asadero Angus Bar & Grill
25. Angencia Arjona
    Hardware
26. Gordo's Boatyard
27. Abarratera Market
28. Tacos Asadero La Chispa
29. Movie Theaters
30. Auto Detallado
31. La Luna Meat Market
32. Cruise Ship Terminal
33. Cruiseport Marina
34. Post Office
35. Guadelupe Church
36. Corona Hotel
37. La Palapaloca Bar
38. Hospital
39. Gigante Market
40. Las Conzuelas Restaurant
41. Naval Base
42. Marina Coral & Hotel
43. Quintas Papagayo Hotel &
    El Pelicano Restaurant
44. Super Rapido Market
45. Pemex Gas Station
46. Juarez Monument
47. 3 Heads Monuments
48. Flag Pole
49. La Baguette
50. Tourist Information
51. Compu Club
52. El Rey Sol Restaurant
53. Villalva Yacht Services
54. Tornillos Alvarado
    Hardware
55. Bronco's Steakhouse
56. Temo Tire Shop
57. Danny's Upholstrey
58. 99 Cent Store
59. Doctor Ortiz Dentist
60. San Martin Pharmacy
61. Centro Social Y Cultural
62. Bodegas Santo Tomas
63. Napa Auto Parts
64. Avalos Tire Shop
65. Industrial Electrical
    Supply
66. Air Conditioning Repair
67. Tourist Information
68. Angus Steakhouse
69. Hotel Playa
70. Hotel Bahia
71. Restaurant Pekin
72. ixtle Embroidery

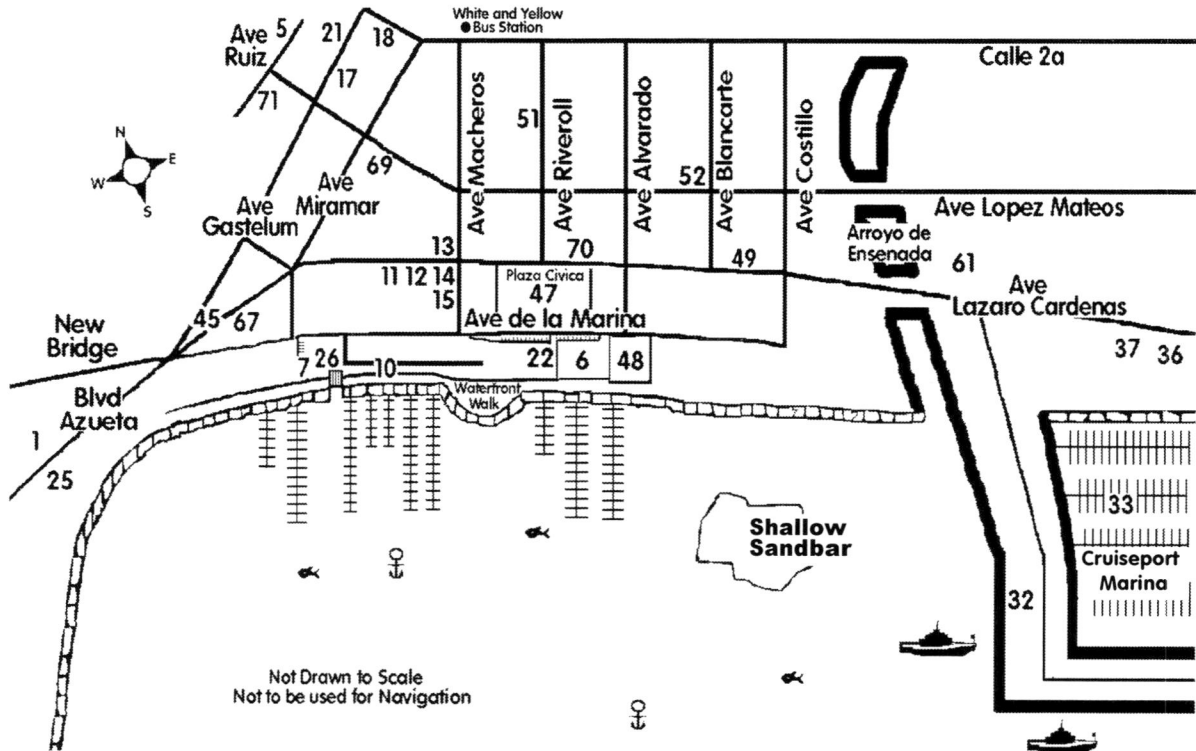

Ensenada Waterfront Site Map

Ave Ruiz 5 21 18
White and Yellow Bus Station
Calle 2a
17
71
69
Ave Macheros 51
Ave Riveroll
Ave Alvarado
Ave Blancarte 52
Ave Costillo
N
W E
S
Ave Miramar
Ave Gastelum
13
70
Plaza Civica
Ave Lopez Mateos
Arroyo de Ensenada
New Bridge
11 12 14
15
47
Ave de la Marina
49
61
Ave Lazaro Cardenas
45 67
37 36
Blvd Azueta
7 26
10
22 6 48
Waterfront Walk
1
25
Shallow Sandbar
Cruiseport Marina
33
32
Not Drawn to Scale
Not to be used for Navigation

1. Port Captain & Immigration
5. Hussong's Cantina
6. Baja Naval
7. Fish Market
10. Gordo's, Juanito's, & Sergio's Sportfishing
11. Baja Cellular
12. Pizza Hut
13. McDonalds
14. Mini Mart Liquor Store
15. Alfonso's Pizza
17. Gigante Market
18. Tortilleria Renteria
21. Panaderia La Mexican
22. Caliente Sportsbook
25. Angencia Arjona Hardware
26. Gordo's Boatyard
32. Cruise Ship Terminal
33. Cruiseport Marina
36. Corona Hotel
37. La Palapaloca Bar
45. Pemex Gas Station
47. 3 Heads Monuments
48. Flag Pole
49. La Baguette
51. Compu Club
52. El Rey Sol Restaurant
61. Centro Social Y Cultural
67. Tourist Information
69. Hotel Playa
70. Hotel Bahia
71. Restaurant Pekin

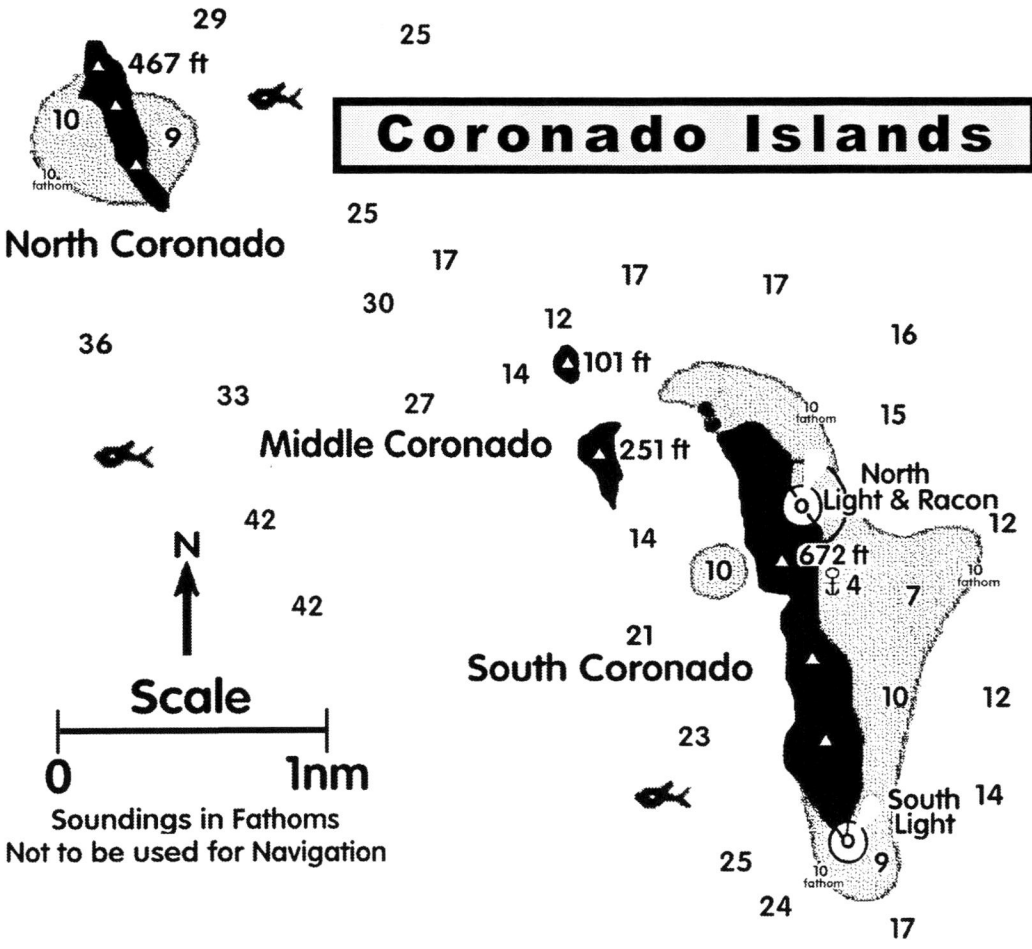

Coronado Islands

29

25

467 ft

North Coronado

10

9

10
fathom

25

17

17

17

30

16

36

12

14 101 ft

15

33

27

Middle Coronado

251 ft

10
fathom

North
Light & Racon

42

14

10

672 ft

12

N

10
4

7

10
fathom

42

Scale

21

South Coronado

10

12

0   1nm

Soundings in Fathoms
Not to be used for Navigation

23

14

South
Light

25

9

24

10
fathom

17

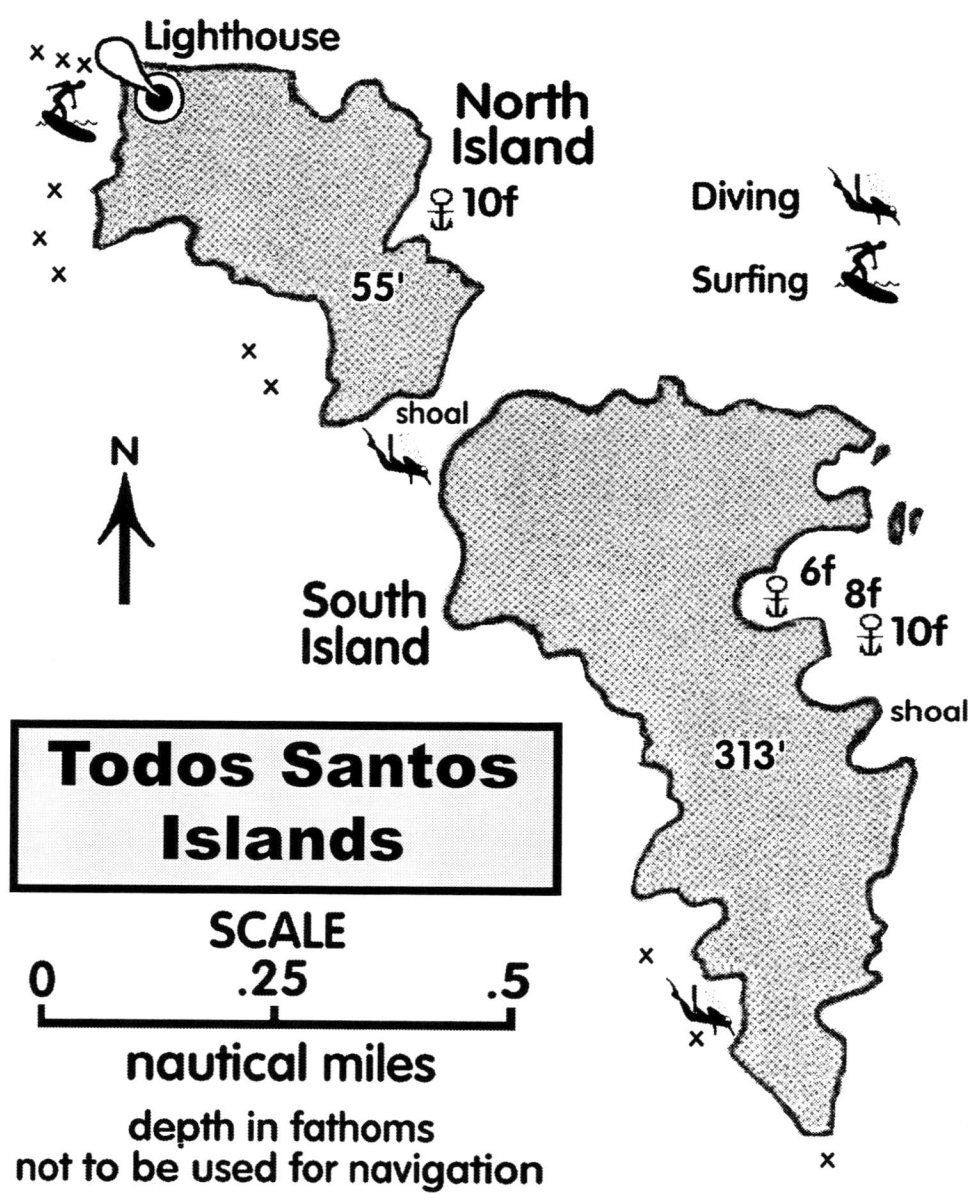

Lighthouse

North Island

♀ 10f

Diving

Surfing

55'

shoal

N

South Island

6f 8f
♀ 10f

shoal

313'

Todos Santos Islands

SCALE
0   .25   .5

nautical miles

depth in fathoms
not to be used for navigation

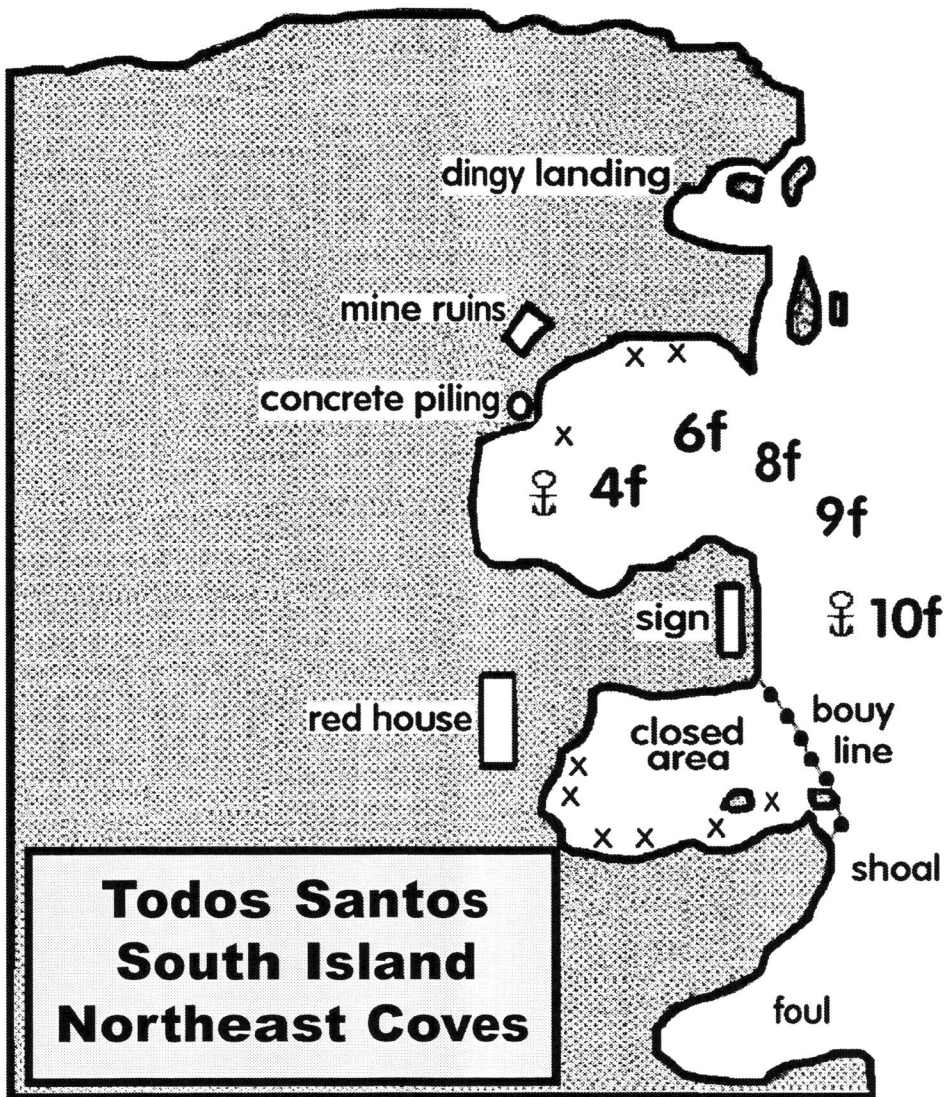

dingy landing

mine ruins

concrete piling

x x

x

6f

8f

♀ 4f

9f

♀ 10f

sign

red house

bouy
line

closed
area

x

x

x

shoal

x x

x

x

foul

**Todos Santos
South Island
Northeast Coves**

not to be used for navigation
many snags encountered when anchoring
soundings in fathoms

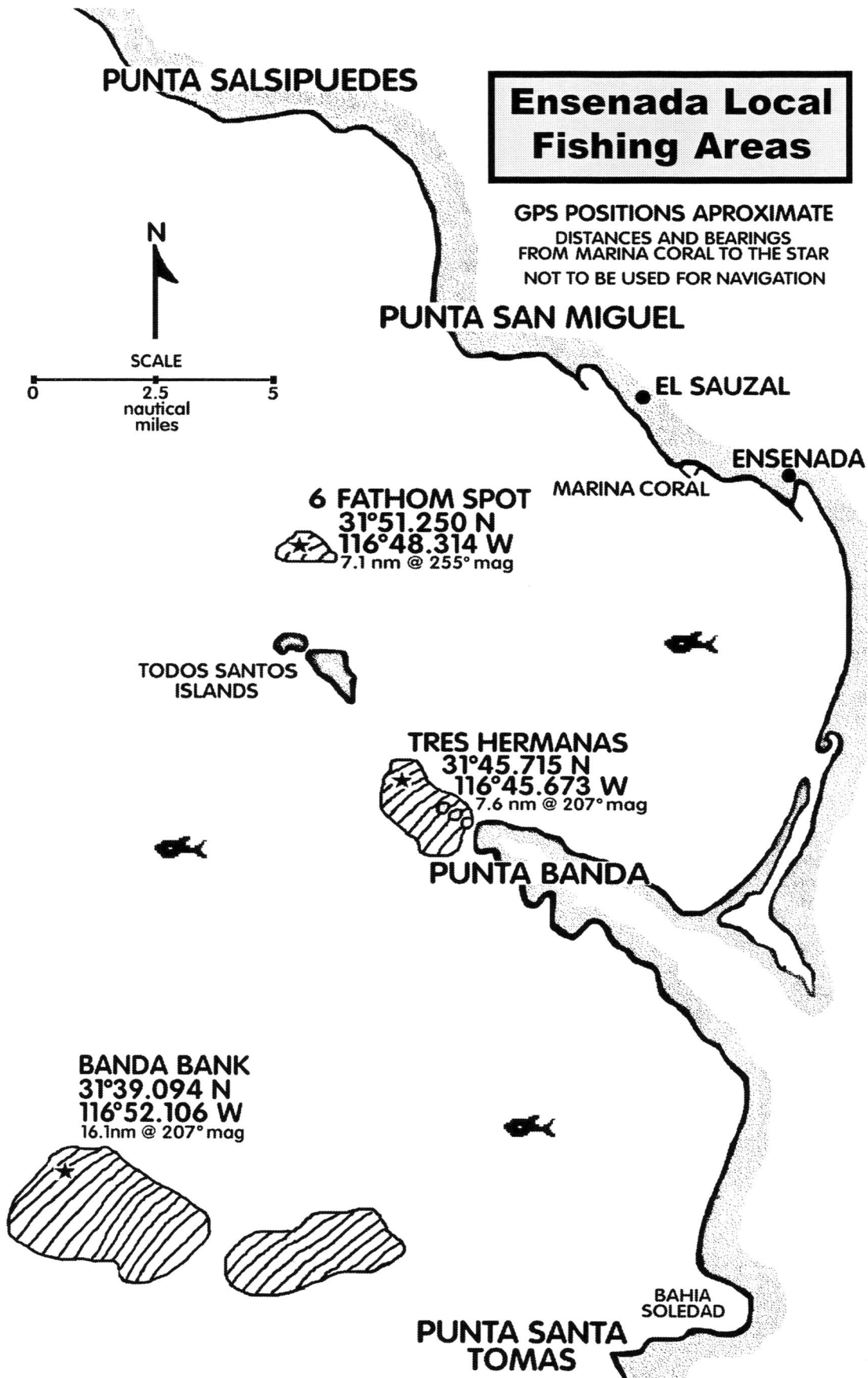

PUNTA SALSIPUEDES

Ensenada Local Fishing Areas

GPS POSITIONS APROXIMATE

DISTANCES AND BEARINGS
FROM MARINA CORAL TO THE STAR

NOT TO BE USED FOR NAVIGATION

N

SCALE

0   2.5   5
nautical
miles

PUNTA SAN MIGUEL

EL SAUZAL

ENSENADA

MARINA CORAL

6 FATHOM SPOT
31°51.250 N
116°48.314 W
7.1 nm @ 255° mag

TODOS SANTOS
ISLANDS

TRES HERMANAS
31°45.715 N
116°45.673 W
7.6 nm @ 207° mag

PUNTA BANDA

BANDA BANK
31°39.094 N
116°52.106 W
16.1nm @ 207° mag

BAHIA
SOLEDAD

PUNTA SANTA
TOMAS

Baja Naval Marina
Coral Marina
Cruiseport Marina

Penasco Marina

Real Marina
San Carlos Marina

Santa Cruz Bay Marina
Abaroa Marina
Palmira Marina
La Paz Marina

El Cid Marina
Mazatlan Marina

Cabo San Lucas Marina

Paradise Village Marina
Vallarta Marina
North Vallarta Marina

Puerto de la Navidad Marina
Las Hadas Marina(Manzanillo)

Ixtapa Marina
Puerto Mia Marina

Acapulco Marina
Acapulco Yacht Club

Darsena Santa Cruz Marina
(Huatulco)

Mexican Marinas

Marinas	Web Sites and E-mail Addresses
Acapulco Marina	www.clubdeyatesaca.com.mx
Cabo San Lucas Marina	www.cabomarina.com.mx
La Paz Marina	www.marinadelapaz.com
El Cid Marina	www.elcid.com
Ixtapa Marina	www.sidek.com.mx/dev/marina_ixt.html
Las Hadas Marina	www.brisas.com.mx/Manzanillo/web/marina.html
Mazatlan Marina	www.sidek.com.mx/dev/marina_mzt.html
Palmira Marina	www.marinapalmira.com
Paradise Village Marina	www.paradisevillage.com
Puerto de La Navidad Marina	www.islanavidad.com
Real Marina	www.marinareal.net
San Carlos Marina	www.marinasancarlos.com
Dársena Santa Cruz Marina	pto@huatulco.net.mx
North Vallarta Marina	marvta@prodigy.net.mx
Vallarta Marina	marvta@prodigy.net.mx
Santa Cruz Bay Marina	santacruz1@prodigy.net.mx
Peñasco Marina	sitmac@prodigy.net.mx

Important Ensenada Phone Numbers

Mexico Country Code: 011
Ensenada Area Code: 646
Police: 060
Red Cross: 066
Fire Department: 068
State Police: 061
Federal Police: 112
Green Angels Highway Help: 176-46-75
Highway Patrol: 176-13-11
SSSTE Hospital: 176-52-76
INSS Hospital: 178-87-00
State Office of Tourism: 172-30-22
Customs: 174-08-97
Immigration: 174-01-64

Spanish Glossery

Around Town

ABARROTES	GROCERIES
ABIERTO	OPEN
ACEITE DE COCINA	COOKING OIL
BANCO	BANK
BASTANTE	ENOUGH
BASURA	TRASH
CAMINO/CALLE	ROAD
CERRADO	CLOSED
CERVESA	BEER
COMESTIBLES	FOOD
DERECHA	RIGHT
FARMACIA	DRUGSTORE
HIELO	ICE
IZQUIERDA	LEFT
LICOR	LIQUOR
MARISCOS	SHELLFISH
MAS/MENOS	MORE/LESS
MERCADO	MARKET
PANADERIA	BAKERY
POLICIA	POLICE
TIENDA	STORE
VERDURAS	VEGETABLES

Body Parts

BRAZO	ARM
CABEZA	HEAD
CODERA	HIP
CODO	ELBOW
CUERPO	BODY
ESPALDA	BACK
HOMBRO	SHOULDER
MANO	HAND
MUNECA	WRIST
OJO	EYE
PIE	FOOT
PIERNA	ELBOW
RODILLA	KNEE

Climate

ASOLEADO	SUNNY
CALIENTE	HOT
CHUBASCO	SQUAL
CIELO	SKY
CLARO	CLEAR
FRIO	COLD
HURACAN	HURRICANE
LLUVIA	RAIN
NIEBLA	FOG
NUBE	CLOUDS
NUBLADO	CLOUDY
TEMPESTAD	STORM
VIENTO	WIND

Greetings and Phrases

BIENVENIDOS ABORDO	WELCOME ABOARD
BUENA SUERTE	GOOD LUCK
BUENOS DIAS	GOOD DAY
BUENAS NOCHES	GOOD EVENING
BUENAS TARDES	GOOD AFTERNOON
CUANTO	HOW MUCH
DE NADA	YOU ARE WELCOME
DONDE ESTA	WHERE IS IT?
DONDE VA	WHERE ARE YOU GOING?
GRACIAS	THANK YOU
HABLA INGLES	DO YOU SPEAK ENGLISH?
HOLA	HELLO
LLAME A LA POLICIA	CALL THE POLICE
MUY BONITA	VERY BEAUTIFUL
MUY PELIGROSA	VERY DANGEROUS
NO HABLA ESPANOL	I DO NOT SPEAK SPANISH
POR FAVOR	PLEASE
QUE HORA ES	WHAT TIME IS IT?
QUE PASO	WHAT'S HAPPENING?
QUE PROFUNDIDAD	HOW DEEP?
SALUT	BLESS YOU
SIENTESE POR FAVOR	PLEASE SIT DOWN

Boat Terms

SABORDO	ABOARD
ADUANA	CUSTOMS
AGUA	WATER
ALTO/BAJO	HIGH/LOW
ARRECIFE	REEF
ARRIVAR	ARRIVE
ARROYO	STREAM/GULLY
AYUDA	HELP
BAHIA	BAY
BAJA	LOWER
BARCO	BOAT
BOCA	MOUTH/ENTRANCE
BOMBA	PUMP
BOYA	BOUY
BUCEAR	DIVE
CABO	CAPE
CALETA	COVE
CANAL	CHANNEL
CAPITAN DEL PUERTO	CAPTAIN OF THE PORT
CAPITANO(A)	CAPTAIN
CLARO	CLEAR
CORRIENTE	CURRENT
DIESEL	DIESEL
ENSENADA	COVE/SMALL BAY
ENTRADA	ENTRANCE
ESCOLAR/BARAR	AGROUND
ESTE	EAST
ESTERO	INLET/ESTUARY
FARALLON	CLIFF
FARRO	LIGHTHOUSE
FONDO	BOTTOM
GASOLINA	GASOLINE
GAZ	PROPANE
GOLFO	GULF
HONDO/BAJO	DEEP/SHALLOW
HUNDIENDO	SINKING
HURACANO	HURRICANE
ISLA(S)	ISLAND(S)

Boat Terms Continued

ISLOTE(S)	INLET(S)
LAGUNA	LAGOON
LATITUD	LATITUDE
LLEGADA	ARRIVAL
LONGITUD	LONGITUDE
MAR	SEA
MAREA	TIDE
MECHANICO	MECHANIC
MESA	MESA/PLATEAU
MIGRATION	IMMIGRATION
MONTANA	MOUNTAIN
MORRO	HEADLAND/CLIFF
MOTOR	ENGINE
NIEBLA	FOG
NORTE	NORTH
NUBE/NUBLADO	CLOUDS/CLOUDY
OCEANO	OCEAN
OESTE	WEST
ONDAS/OLAS	WAVES
PANGA	SMALL FISHING BOAT
PESCADO	FISH
PICACHO	SMALL PEAK
PICO	PEAK
PIEDRA	ROCK
PILOTA	PILOT
PLAYA	BEACH
PUERTO	PORT/HARBOR
PUNTA	POINT
REMOLCAR	TOW
RIO	RIVER
ROCA(S)	ROCK(S)
SANTA	SAINT
SIERRA	MOUNTAIN RANGE
SOGA/CUERDA	ROPE
VELA	SAIL
VIENTO	WIND

Road Terms

AL PASO	DEAD SLOW
ALTO	STOP
APARCAMIENTO	CAR PARK
ATENCION	CAUTION
AUTOPISTA	MOTORWAY
AVENIDA	AVENUE
BIFURCACION	ROAD FORK
CALLE	STREET
CASETA DE COBRO	TOLL BOOTH
CEDA AL PASO	GIVE WAY
CUIDADO	CAUTION
CUOTA	TOLL
CURVA PELIGROSA	DANGEROUS CURVE
DESVIO	DIVERSION
GRUA	TOW AWAY SERVICE
LIBRE	FREE
OBRAS	ROAD WORKS
PASO PROHIBIDO	NO ENTRY
PEATONES	PEDESTRIANS
PELIGRO	DANGER
PLAYA	BEACH
PROHIBIDO ESTACIONAR	NO PARKING
PROHIBIDO REBASAR	NO OVERTAKING
UN SENTIDO	ONE WAY STREET

Traveling by Bus or Train

ANDEN	PLATFORM
APEADERO	HALT
BILLETE	TICKET
CAMION/AUTOBUS	BUS/COACH
EMPALME	JUNCTION
EQUIPAJE	LUGGAGE/BAGGAGE
ESTACION	STATION
HORARIO DE TRENOS	TRAIN TIMETABLE
LLEGADA	ARRIVAL
NO FUMADORES	NO SMOKING AREA
PARADA	STOP
PRECIO/IMPORTE	FARE
PRIMERA CLASE	FIRST CLASS
REVISOR	TICKET COLLECTOR
SALA DE ESPERA	WAITING ROOM
SALIDA	DEPARTURE
SEGUNDA CLASE	SECOND CLASS
TAQUILLA DE BILLETES	TICKET-WINDOW
TREN	TRAIN

Mexican Ports of Entry

Following is a list of ports other then Ensenada throughout Mexico where clearance into the country is possible. If you choose to spend your time in another part of Mexico during your offshore delivery period, this will suffice as qualifying you for tax exemption. But the further you are from your boat may make the actual time spent on your boat more difficult. And the fulfillment of your duties to qualify you for tax exemption include spending much of the time offshore residing on your boat and using it in the foreign country. This is why we have focused the content of this book on the Ensenada area due to the fact that its proximity to California is so convenient for spending time on your boat while collecting the receipts needed to prove your offshore time on your boat. We have enjoyed our time spent in Ensenada and hope you do also.

Cabo San Lucas, Baja
Cedros, Baja
San Carlos, Sonora
Loreto, Baja
Santa Rosalia, Baja
Guaymas, Sonora
Topolobamba, Sinaloa
Mazatlan, Sinaloa
San Blas, Nayarit
Chacala, Nayarit
Puerto Vallarta, Jalisco
Manzanillo, Guerero
Zihuatanejo, Guerero
Acapulco, Guerero
Puerto Angel, Oaxaca
Salina Cruz, Oaxaca

LOCAL COLOR

Flowers and sculptures surrounding the
Marina Coral pool, an artistic
addition to the beauty of the
natural environment.

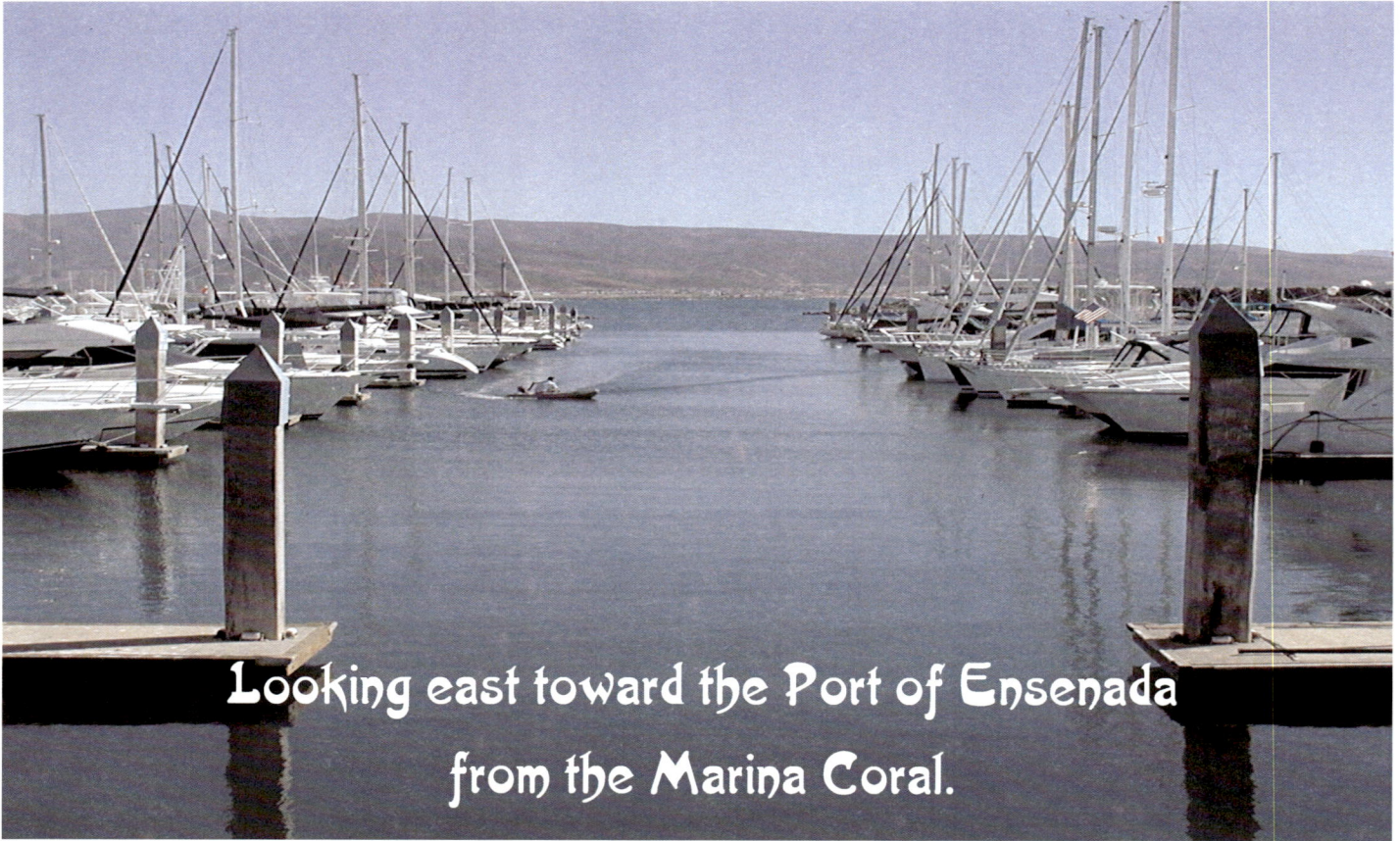

Looking east toward the Port of Ensenada
from the Marina Coral.

Clear skies enhance a winter sunset.

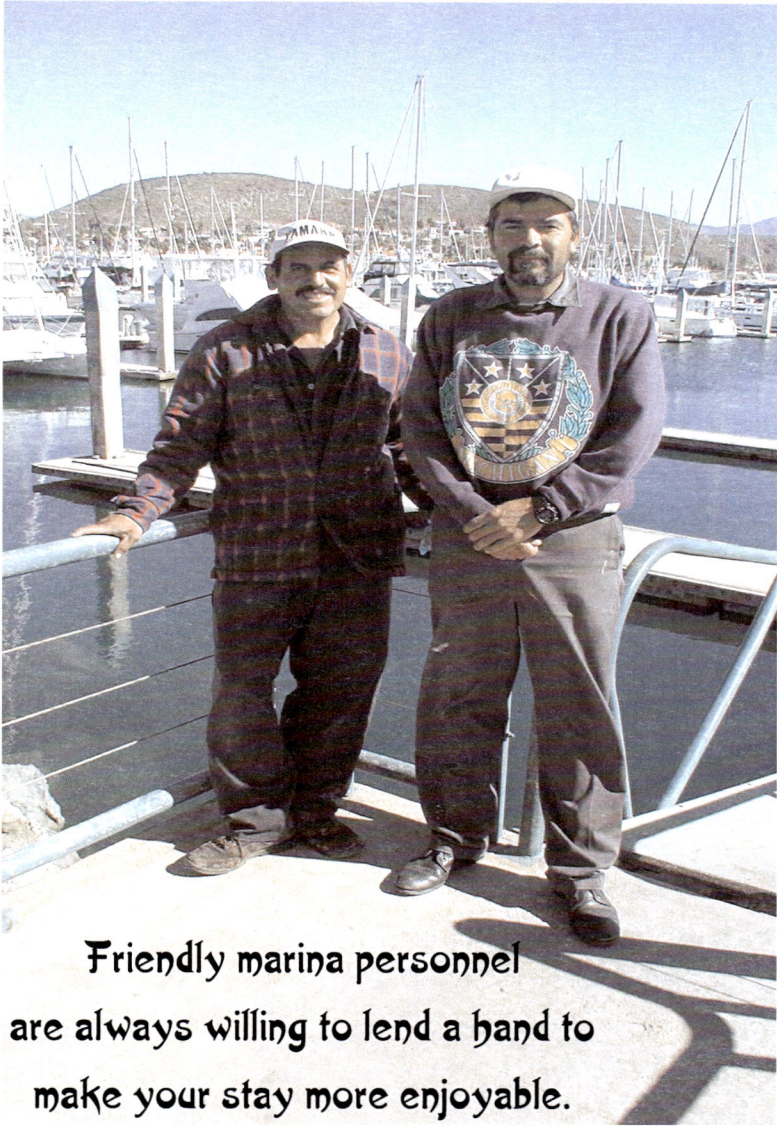

Friendly marina personnel
are always willing to lend a hand to
make your stay more enjoyable.

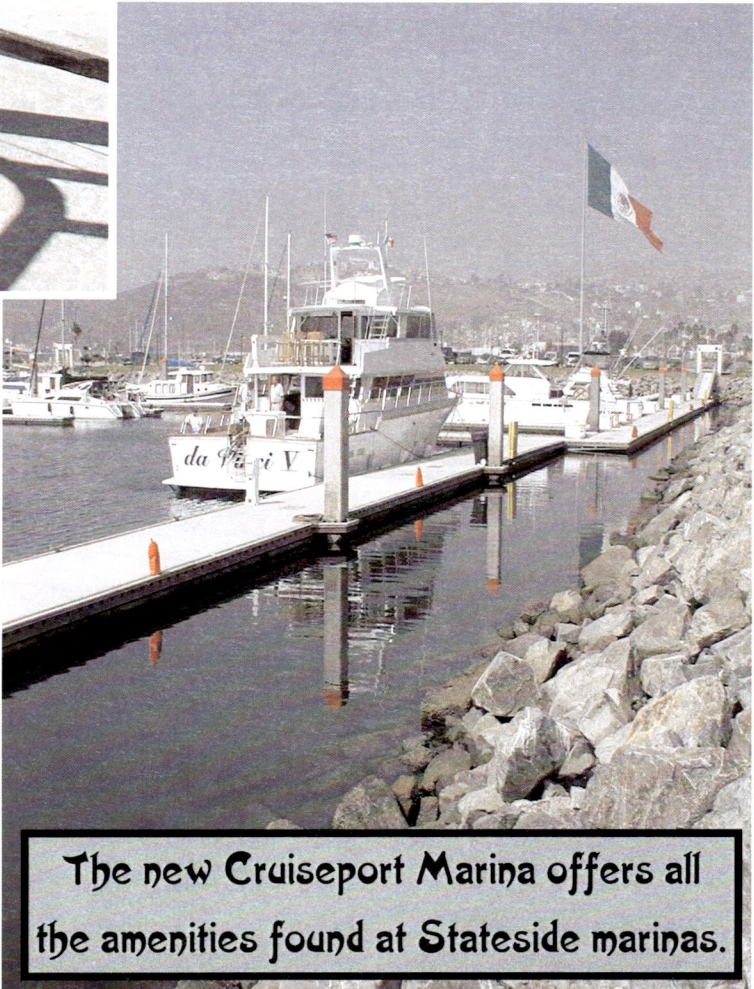

The new Cruiseport Marina offers all
the amenities found at Stateside marinas.

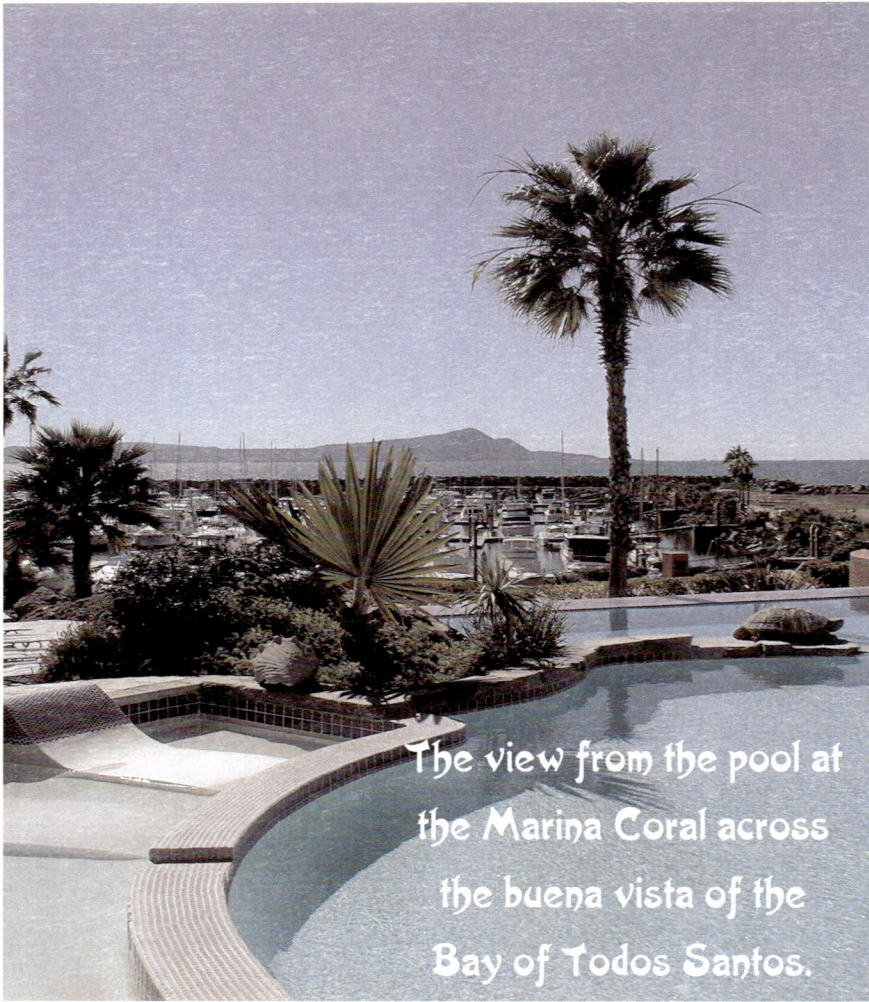

The view from the pool at the Marina Coral across the buena vista of the Bay of Todos Santos.

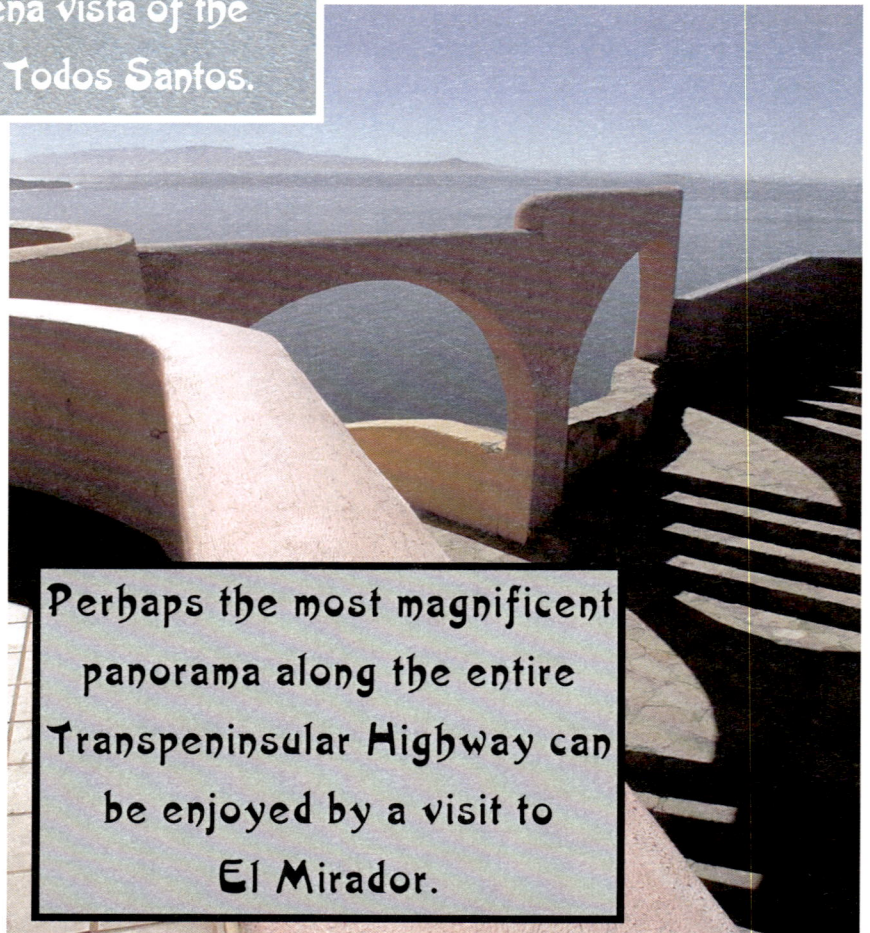

Perhaps the most magnificent panorama along the entire Transpeninsular Highway can be enjoyed by a visit to El Mirador.

A windy afternoon at K-38.

Simple seaside retreat.

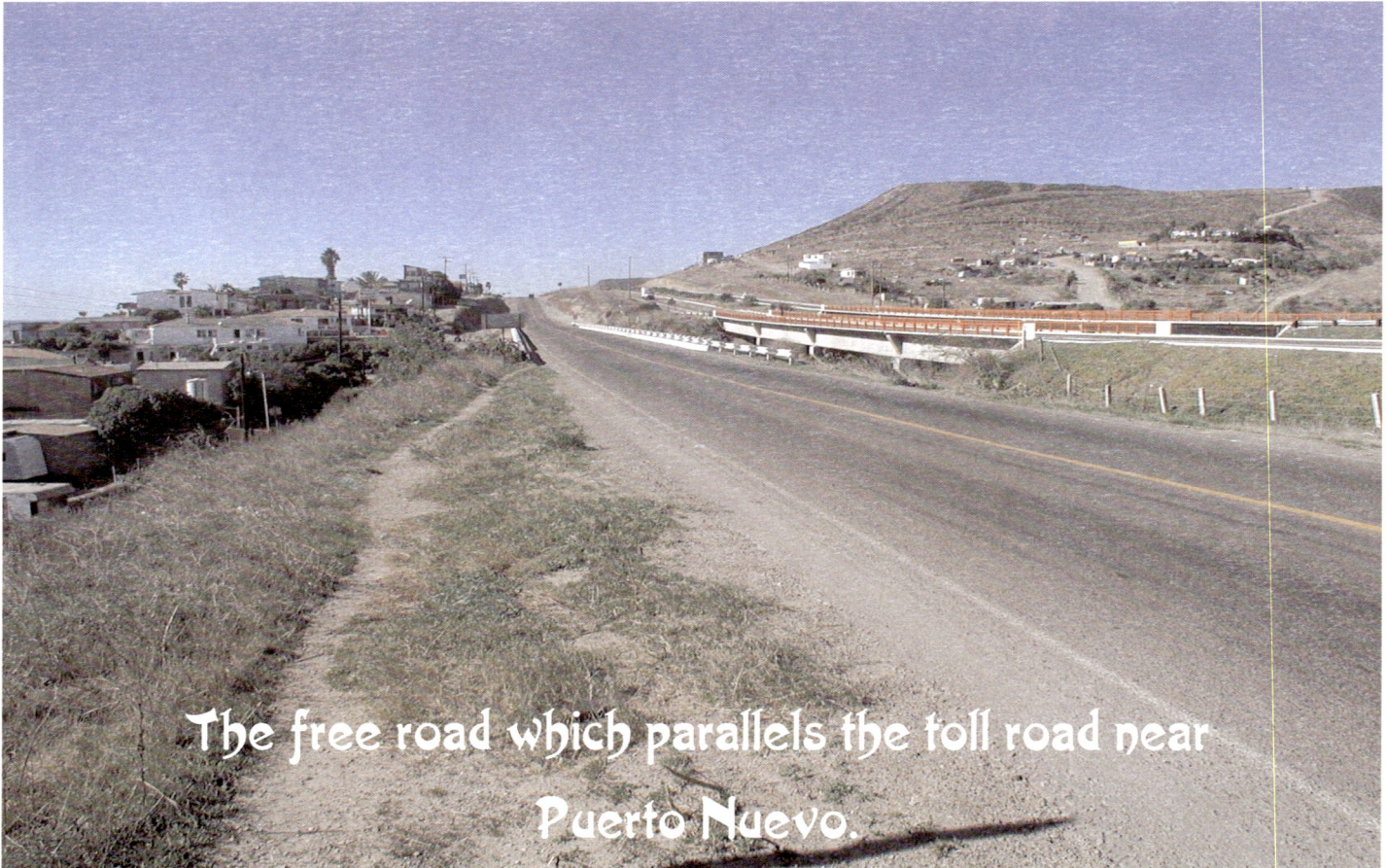

The free road which parallels the toll road near Puerto Nuevo.

Our favorite stop en route to Ensenada, Tamales Las Gaviotas.

Easily understood road signs direct your travels
to the 90 Day Yacht Club.

A lazy day for the horses waiting to run with you
on the beach.

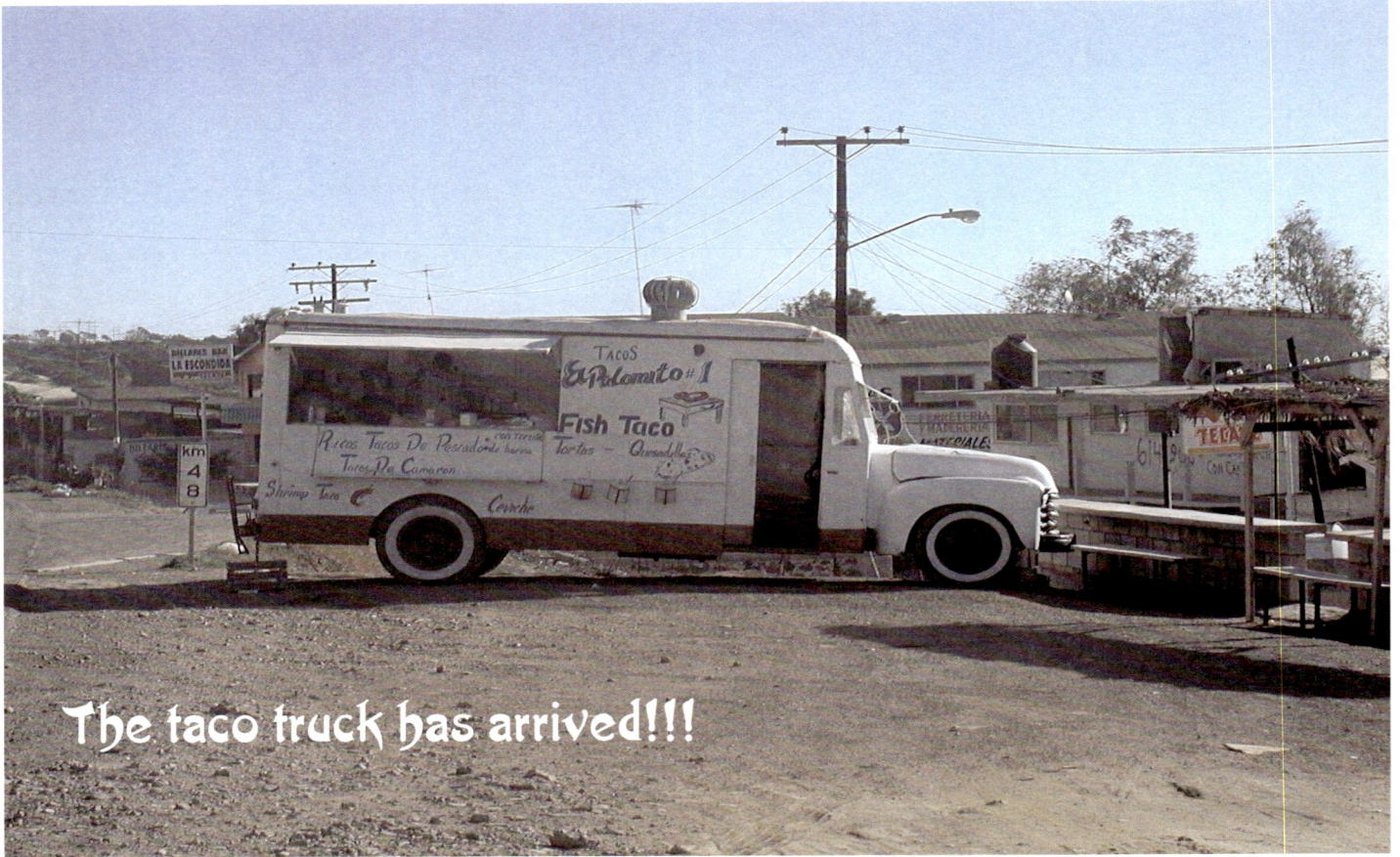

The taco truck has arrived!!!

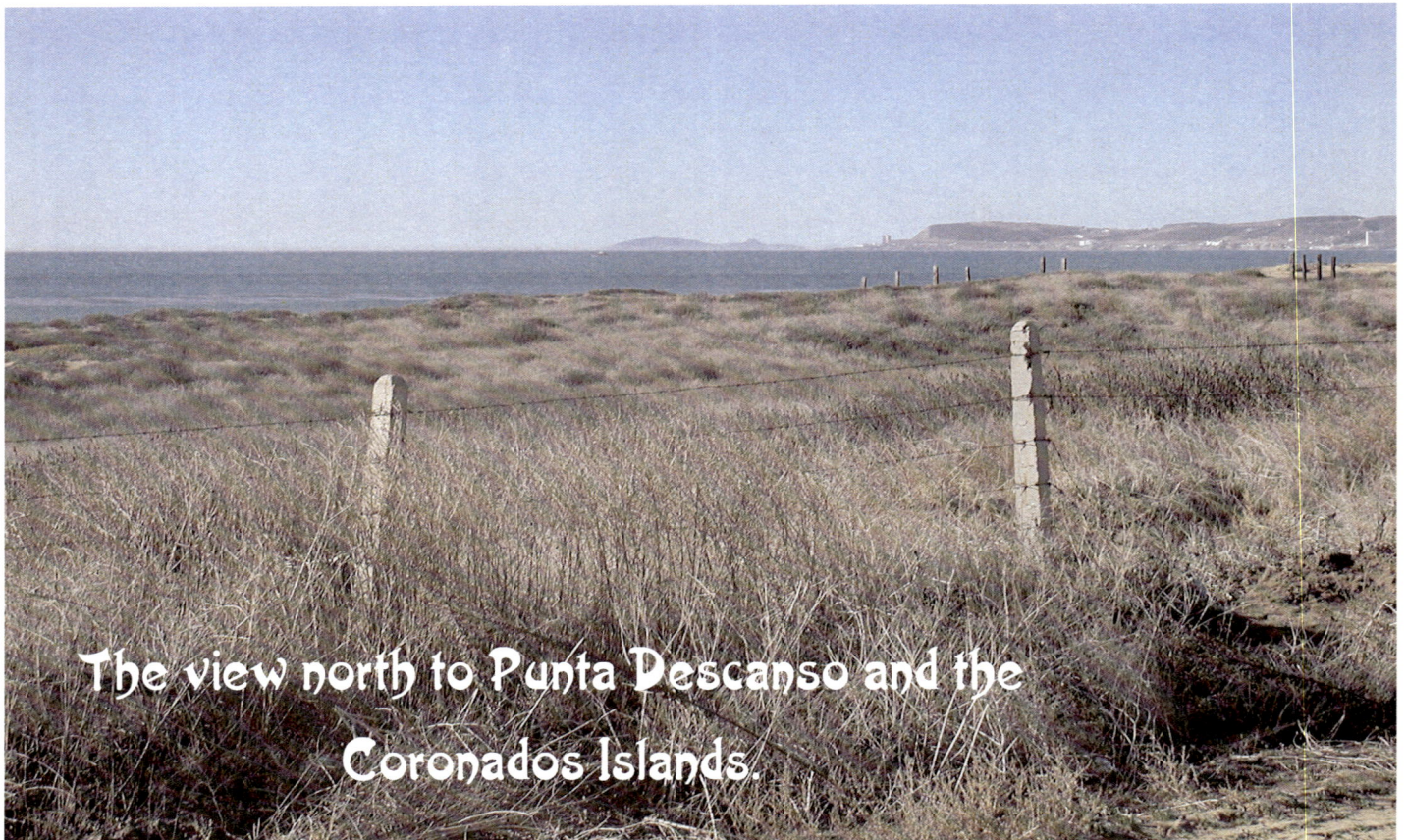

The view north to Punta Descanso and the Coronados Islands.

Sunset entry...

...to the Port of Ensenada.

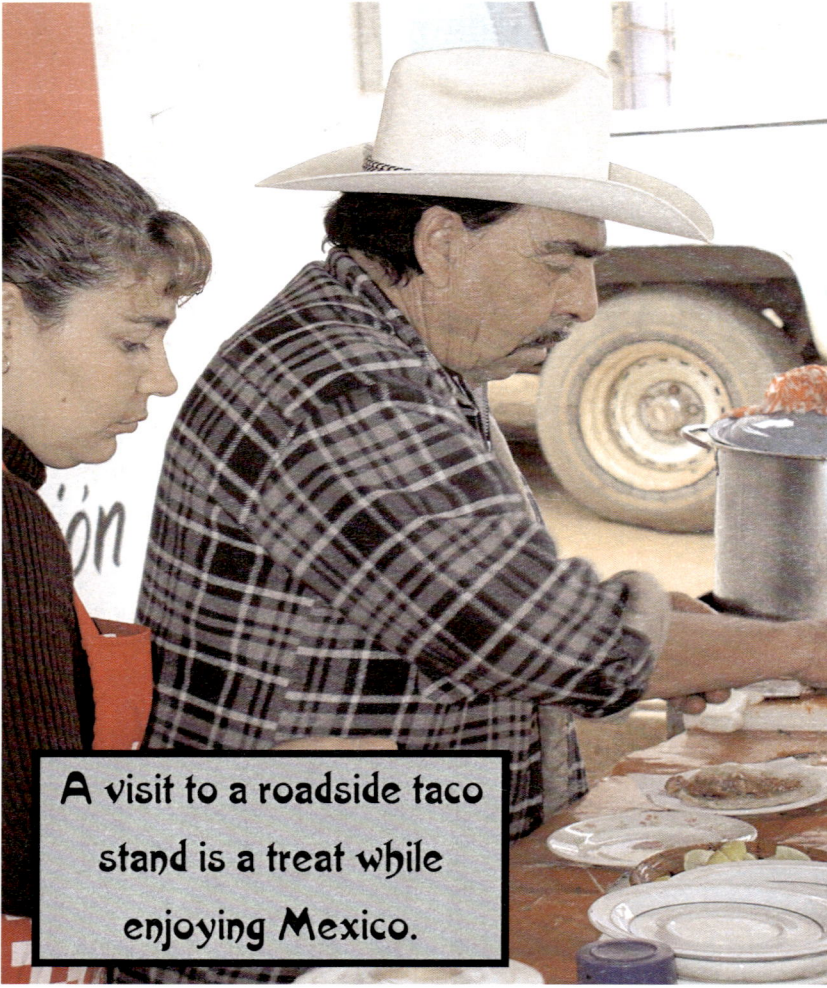

A visit to a roadside taco stand is a treat while enjoying Mexico.

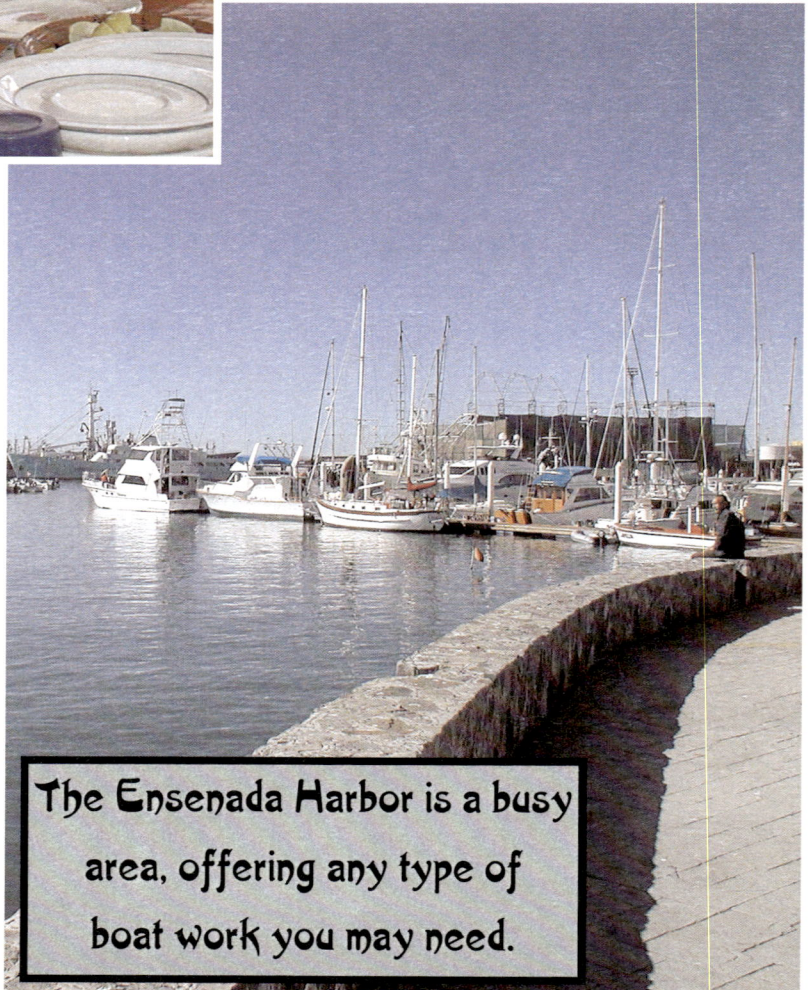

The Ensenada Harbor is a busy area, offering any type of boat work you may need.

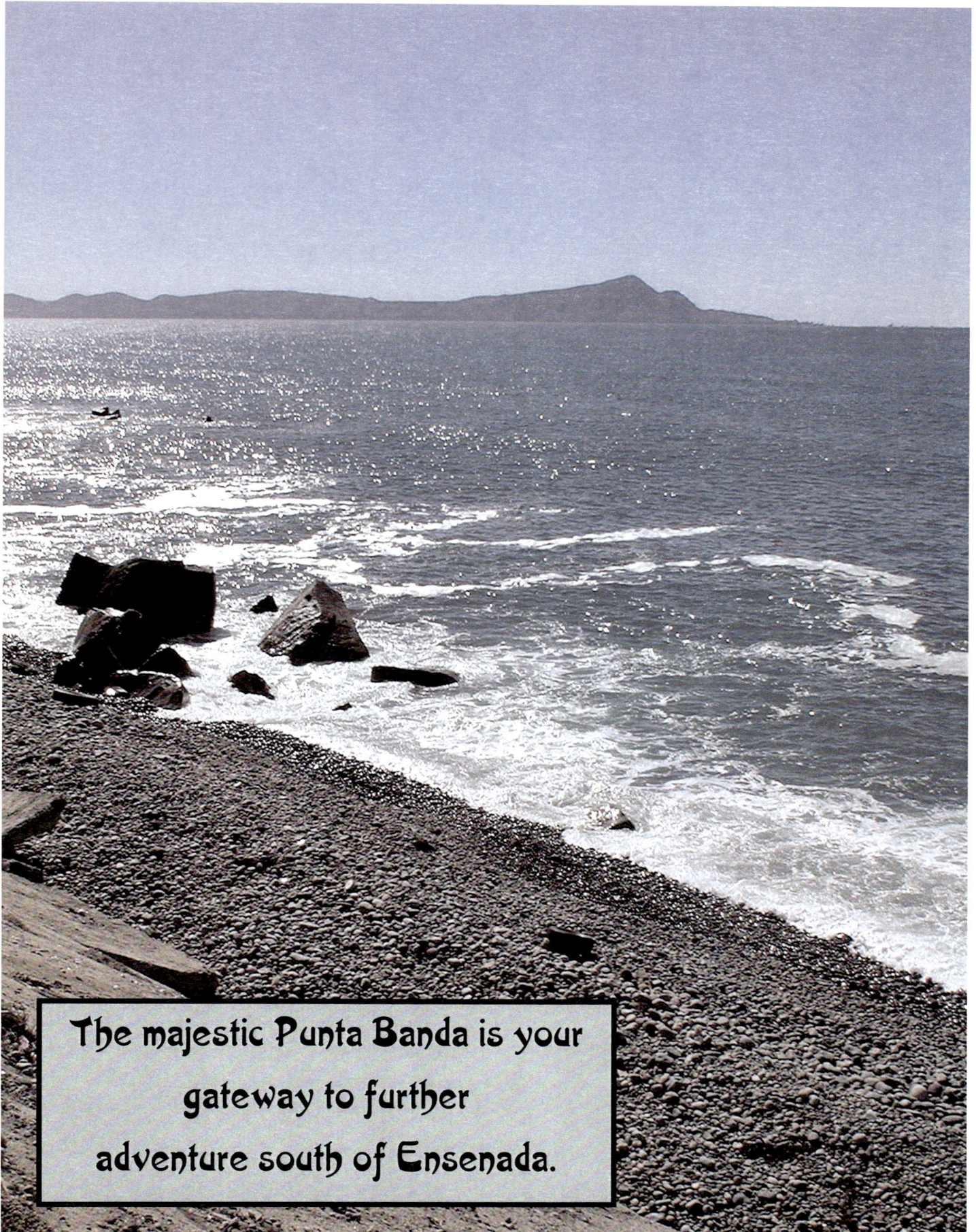

The majestic Punta Banda is your gateway to further adventure south of Ensenada.

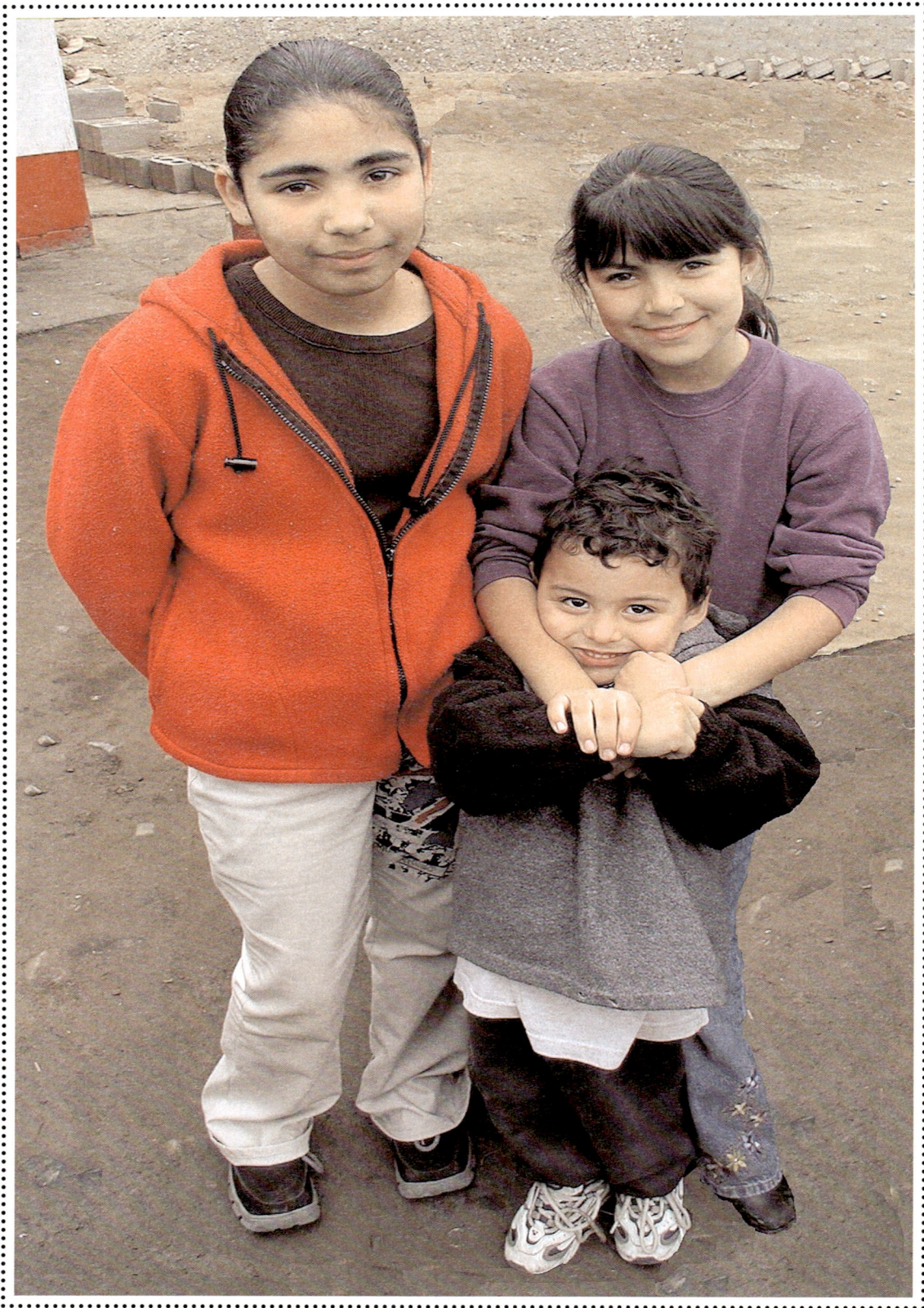

Come visit us soon, por favor!

INDEX

THE BEGINNING
OF YOUR TRUE TRAVELS
AND
THE END
OF
THIS BOOK

A Testimonial from a Boater About
The 90 Day Yacht Club Guide to Ensenada

Dear Captain Lonnie Ryan,

I wanted to let you know how much I enjoyed and appreciated your book. My wife and I put it to good use recently when we took our first boat trip from San Diego to Ensenada. Originally we had planned to make the trip with two friends who have considerably more sea experience than we do. Unfortunately, they had to cancel at the last minute. My wife and I discussed whether we should attempt the trip alone. We had a certain amount of anxiety because we had never traveled by sea to Ensenada. Our previous boating experience was limited to local fishing trips and a trip to Catalina. Since I had already made reservations at the Coral Marina, we decided to give it a go. We started our trip about 4:00 a.m. at Pt. Loma, buoy 5, and were in fog and heavy marine layer almost immediately. Thanks to our ability to set the auto pilot by the GPS waypoints described in the book, we were able to concentrate on using our radar to stay out of harms way. Although our visibility wasn't great, the sea was smooth as glass. We arrived safely at the Coral Marina about 10:00 a. m. and were greeted warmly by the dock hands who helped tie up the boat, and the marina office staff who squared away our paperwork with the Port Captain and Immigration. We celebrated our arrival by having drinks and lunch at the Gastelum 57, a restaurant you recommend in the book. This was a very nice place to dine. The food and service were excellent. Our return to San Diego mirrored our trip to Ensenada. We encountered lots of fog, marine layer, poor visibility, but calm seas. However, by this time we were feeling pretty cocky because "we had already been there, done that." We were feeling like seasoned mariners by the time we arrived at the Port of San Diego Customs dock. We arrived home safely and with considerably more confidence than when we started.

Lonnie, I commend you for writing a great book. It is very readable and has great information that would help anyone not acquainted with Ensenada. Everything included in the book, from the article about the fear factor, which we certainly experienced, to the charts and maps were extremely helpful.

Best wishes for success with your book.
Gene and Irene Newton,
Former educators now retired.